THE JOYS OF
ALMOND MILK

THE JOYS OF ALMOND MILK

Delicious Recipes for the Dairy-Free

INSTRUCTABLES.COM

Edited and Introduced by

Nicole Smith

Skyhorse Publishing

Skyhorse Publishing books may be purchased in bulk at special discounts for sales promotion, corporate gifts, fund-raising, or educational purposes. Special editions can also be created to specifications. For details, contact the Special Sales Department, Skyhorse Publishing, 307 West 36th Street, 11th Floor, New York, NY 10018 or info@skyhorsepublishing.com.

Skyhorse® and Skyhorse Publishing® are registered trademarks of Skyhorse Publishing, Inc.®, a Delaware corporation.

Visit our website at www.skyhorsepublishing.com.

10 9 8 7 6 5 4 3 2 1

Library of Congress Cataloguing-in-Publication Data is available on file.

ISBN: 978-1-62914-800-7
Ebook ISBN: 978-1-62914-809-0

Printed in China

TABLE OF CONTENTS

Introduction

Almond milk is a delicious alternative to cow's milk. Not only does it add a great flavor to every recipe, but it also is incredibly easy to make!

To start things off, we are going to show you exactly how to make your own almond milk and condensed almond milk. From there we will begin with delicious breakfast recipes made with almond milk including Banana Split Pancakes and Homemade Breakfast Cereal. If you usually skip breakfast, you won't anymore after trying these recipes; and the goodness won't stop there!

Follow along as the chefs from the Instructables community show you how to enhance your lunches and dinners with delicious recipes for chicken wings with hot sauce, zucchini bread, and a vegan baked potato soup!

Did you know you could make a delicious chocolate mousse using almond milk and an avocado? We'll show you how along with other amazing desserts to end a perfect meal. The recipes from this book are contributed by the members of the Instructables community. With nothing but an ordinary kitchen and a few ingredients, they are able to pull together amazing meals. Join them and learn *The Joys of Almond Milk*.

—Nicole Smith
(Penolopy Bulnick)

FROM SCRATCH

Almond Milk

by ChrysN

http://www.instructables.com/id/Almond-Milk/

Here is a great alternative to cow, soy, and rice milk, which is tasty and really easy to make yourself. You can drink it straight or add it to smoothies, and it's excellent on cereal!

INGREDIENTS

- 1 cup skinless (blanched)* almonds, whole or ground
- 3 cups water filtered + water to soak

*If you can only find almonds with the skin still on, your milk will have little bits of almond skin floating around. If this bothers you, you can blanch them.

EQUIPMENT

- blender
- sieve or cheesecloth
- bowl
- pitcher with lid (to store milk when done)
- spatula
- measuring cup

Step 1: Blanching

If your almonds do not have the skin on them, you can skip this step.

Pour boiling water over almonds to cover them. After about 1 minute, drain and rinse under cold water. Pat dry and slip the skin off.

Step 2: Soaking Overnight

Place 1 cup of almonds into a bowl and add water (use filtered water if you would like) so that it covers almonds. Soak in fridge overnight if you can or for a minimum of 4 hours.

Step 3: Blend

The following day, drain water from the bowl of almonds. Place almonds in a blender, add 3 cups of water (again you can use filtered water here), and blend until smooth. This can take 1 to 2 minutes or so, depending on your blender.

It is ready when it is more or less homogeneous and the almond particles are quite fine.

Step 4: Strain and Serve

Pour from blender into a sieve/cheesecloth over a container to collect the milk. If you are using a sieve, take a spatula and squeeze the pulp to get as much liquid out as you can. (If you are using cheesecloth, give it a good squeeze, too.) Don't throw out the pulp as you can use it for baking. After it has been strained, you can drink it as is or you can flavor or sweeten it (see next step). Store in a closed container in the fridge. It will keep up to a week in fridge.

Step 5: Options

Put the milk back into the blender (rinse the blender first). Blend until smooth, and store in a closed container in the fridge. It will keep up to a week in the fridge.

Sweetening

To sweeten you can add any of the following, adjust to taste, and blend again until smooth.

- 1 Tablespoon sugar, honey, or maple syrup
- 1 banana or 2 Tablespoons pitted dates

Flavoring

For flavor you can add vanilla extract, cocoa (or chocolate milk powder), or fruit purée.

Thickening

You can make this a thicker drink by reducing the amount of water you add when blending. Try 2 cups of water instead of 3.

Roasting

You can try roasting your nuts as this brings out their flavor. Before you soak the nuts (step 2), place in the oven at 350°F for about 5 minutes. Keep an eye on them: burned nuts are not so good. Allow to cool and proceed to step 2.

Condensed Almond Milk

by atepinkrose
http://www.instructables.com/id/Condensed-Almond-Milk/

Dairy-free milk is an option, for some even a necessity, but most of the time it is either more expensive or not readily available. DIY is one solution.

INGREDIENTS

- oil
- 2 cups of almond milk
- ⅔ cup of sugar or honey
- 1 teaspoon of vanilla
- 1 dash of salt

Step 1: Heat Milk

Grease a saucepan with oil, add the milk, and heat to 120°F.

Step 2: Add Sweetener and Reduce Heat

Once the mixture is hot enough, add the sugar or alternative sweetener, vanilla, and salt, and allow it to boil, stirring frequently. After it reaches a boil, you want to reduce the flame to a simmer, at the lowest setting. Heat for approximately 1 hour, stirring every 15 minutes.

    Let cool.

Step 3: Transfer to Jar

Transfer the mixture to a jar and refrigerate. Use and enjoy!

BREAKFAST

Cranberry Oat Muffins

By savynaturalista

http://www.instructables.com/id/Cranberry-Oat-Muffins/

INGREDIENTS

- 2 stevia packets
- 1 cup cranberries
- ½ cup flour
- ½ cup oats
- ¼ teaspoon salt
- 1 teaspoon cinnamon
- 2 teaspoons baking powder
- 1 egg
- 3 egg whites
- 1 cup coconut sugar
- ½ cup almond milk
- 1 large banana, puréed

Step 1: Preheat and Sift

Preheat oven to 350°F. In a small bowl, mix two packets of stevia with cranberries; sift dry ingredients and set aside.

Step 2: Mix

In a large bowl mix eggs, coconut sugar, almond milk, and banana purée until the mixture is smooth.

Step 3: Combine

Mix dry and wet ingredients until the batter has formed; fold cranberries into the batter.

Step 4: Bake

Line a muffin tin with cupcake liners and place 1 to 2 heaping Tablespoons of batter into each liner. Place in the oven for 30 minutes or until a toothpick stuck in the center of the muffin comes out clean.

Old-Fashioned Pancakes

By savynaturalista
http://www.instructables.com/id/Old-Fashion-Pancakes-
Single-Serving/

INGREDIENTS

- ¼ cup flour
- 1 teaspoon baking powder
- pinch of salt
- 1 Tablespoon sugar
- 1 egg
- 1 Tablespoon vegan butter, melted
- ¼ cup + 3 Tablespoons almond milk

Step 1: Mix Batter

Sift flour, baking powder, salt, and sugar; add egg, melted vegan butter, and milk to the batter and whisk until the batter is smooth. Set aside.

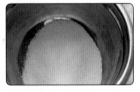

Step 2: Cook and Serve

Grease a pan with oil and set pan on burner at medium heat. Scoop 1–2 Tablespoons of batter into the hot skillet; brown on both sides and serve.

Note: If you'd like to make the egg flavor a little less apparent, you can use 2 egg whites instead of 1 egg or add more sugar or vanilla to the batter. Sifting also helps with the ingredients. If you do not want to sift, make sure your dry ingredients are mixed in well. I also used ¼ cup plus 3 Tablespoons of milk for this batter to make it thin; you do not need the extra milk, but the thinner the batter the more cakes you get.

Banana Split Pancakes

By annahowardshaw

http://www.instructables.com/id/Banana-Split-Pancakes/

MAKES 15 PANCAKES, 6 INCHES IN DIAMETER

Chocolate-, vanilla-, and strawberry-flavored pancakes make up this themed stack. The recipe incorporates the healthier parts of a banana split (fruit and nuts) and purposely avoids getting into chocolate syrup, caramel, or marshmallow. This recipe is more breakfast/brunchy rather than all-out dessert. But one could go crazy and add more toppings or types of pancakes.

INGREDIENTS

- 4 cups flour
- 2 Tablespoons baking powder
- 2 Tablespoons sugar
- 1 teaspoon salt
- 2 eggs
- 3½ cups almond milk*
- 2 Tablespoons sunflower oil

*¼–½ cup may be needed to create even consistency between batters.

EQUIPMENT

- 3 mixing bowls
- electric mixer
- frying pan
- measuring cups/spoons

Additions

- ½ vanilla bean (or 1 teaspoon vanilla extract)
- 1 cup strawberries, diced
- 1 teaspoon lemon zest
- red food coloring (optional)
- 2 Tablespoons cocoa powder

Toppings

- whipped cream or coconut whipped cream
- pecans
- bananas
- maraschino cherries

Step 1: Mix

Mix basic batter in one large bowl.

Step 2: Divide

Divide batter evenly among 3 bowls and add:

Bowl 1: Vanilla bean, removed from pod

Bowl 2: Strawberries, lemon zest, and a couple drops of food coloring, if desired

Bowl 3: Cocoa powder (a little more almond milk may need to be added here)

Step 3: Make Pancakes

Pour batter on heated skillet to make pancakes. Turn when edges are dry and most bubbles have broken.

Step 4: Stack and Add Toppings

Stack a vanilla, chocolate, and strawberry pancake on a plate. Add sliced banana, whipped cream, and nuts. Top with a cherry!

Pumpkin Pancakes

By annahowardshaw

http://www.instructables.com/id/Pumpkin-Pancakes/

A more socially acceptable way to have pumpkin pie for breakfast.

INGREDIENTS

- 1 cup almond meal
- 5 Tablespoons whole wheat flour
- 2 Tablespoon sugar
- 1 teaspoon baking powder
- 1 teaspoon ground cinnamon*
- ½ teaspoon ground nutmeg*
- ¼ teaspoon ground ginger*
- ⅛ teaspoon ground allspice*
- dash of cardamom*
- ¼ teaspoon salt
- 1 cup almond milk
- 1 cup pumpkin purée
- 4 egg yolks
- 3 Tablespoons unsalted butter, melted
- 1 teaspoon vanilla extract
- 3 egg whites

*Or substitute these five ingredients with 2 teaspoons of pumpkin pie spice

EQUIPMENT

- mixing bowls
- skillet
- electric mixer
- whisk
- spatula
- coffee grinder or food processor (if you want to grind your own almond meal)

Step 1: Grind or Purchase

Begin with purchased almond meal, or grind almonds as finely as possible.

Step 2: Mix

In one bowl, mix all dry ingredients.

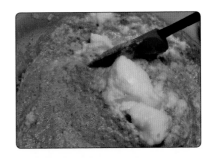

Step 3: Blend and Combine

In a second bowl, thoroughly blend almond milk, pumpkin, egg yolks, butter, and vanilla. Combine wet ingredients into dry.

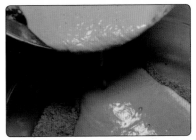

Step 4: Beat and Fold

In a clean, dry bowl, beat egg whites and a pinch of salt until stiff peaks form. Slowly fold egg whites into batter.

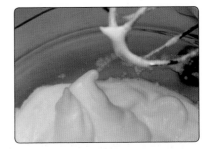

Step 5: Pour

Pour about ⅓ cup of batter on a preheated skillet and flip when edges of pancake are dry and bubbly.

Step 6: Add Topping

Top with ginger syrup, coconut whipped cream, and/or a sprinkle of nutmeg.

Easy Vegan Low-Carb Homemade Breakfast Cereal

By megmaine
http://www.instructables.com/id/Easy-Vegan-low-carb-homemade-breakfast-cereal/

This is one of many uses for the almond meal you will have left over from the process of making almond milk, as detailed in Almond Milk (page 2). Enjoy an easy vegan cold cereal with the almond milk you already made and the almond meal you have left from that process. You can eat it plain, or add dried fruits, other seeds and nuts, fresh fruit, or anything else you please, to make this a convenient, nutrient-packed, high-protein, high-fiber, vegan, soy-free way to start the day.

Step 1: Toast the Almond Meal

Spread the almond meal left over from making almond milk in a half-sheet pan. Place in the oven and bake at 300°F for about an hour, stirring once or twice to determine degree of dryness. You can take it out sooner or leave it in longer depending on your preference for paleness or brownness. All that matters is that it be fully dry, for storage. To avoid using too much energy for one food item, you can toast this on one oven rack, while something else bakes on another.

Step 2: Allow to Cool

When done to your liking, remove the pan from the oven and cool before storing in an airtight container. Refrigeration is not necessary.

Step 3: Pour on the Almond Milk!

And of course, you may be inspired to add sweetener, dried fruits, or other good things to your almond meal cereal.

Step 4: Enjoy!

This is great cold, or it can be heated for a slightly crunchy porridge. It reminds me of "grape nuts" except that this tastes better and does not have the tendency to go mushy or slimy if heated or left in the bowl a while. Diabetics may find this to be a wonderful alternative to the blood-sugar-elevating grain-based cold cereals and high-sugar cow's milk.

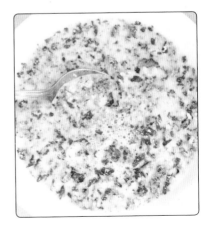

Green Tea Pancakes with Ginger Syrup

By annahowardshaw

http://www.instructables.com/id/Green-Tea-Pancakes-with-Ginger-Syrup/

If you're wondering what to bring to a brunch, these fancy flapjacks will be a hit! They are also great for a weekend afternoon of Netflix.

Decent vegan pancakes have seemed unattainable to me for some time. I tried making them with soy milk and egg substitutes, both resulting in unfortunate texture issues. Almond milk, however, works great! They are a little lighter than a regular pancake but not obviously lacking anything. And the almond flavor goes well with green tea.

The syrup is super spicy, but not stinging or lingering. Enjoy!

INGREDIENTS

- 2 cups sugar
- 1 cup water
- Juice from ½ lemon
- 5 Tablespoons light corn syrup
- 1 cup fresh ginger, sliced

EQUIPMENT

- saucepan
- wooden spoon
- glass bowl

For Storage

- cheesecloth
- glass or plastic container
- funnel

Ginger Syrup

Step 1: Add and Simmer

Add sugar, water, and lemon juice to saucepan and slowly bring to a simmer, stirring regularly with a wooden spoon.

Step 2: Boil, Simmer, and Cool

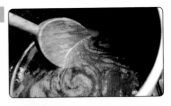

Once sugar is dissolved, carefully mix in corn syrup and add chopped ginger slices. Bring to a boil for 5 minutes. Bring back down to a simmer for 10 more minutes. Allow to cool to room temperature.

Note: To thicken syrup without corn syrup you can use honey. After mixture cools, mix in the honey and heat on low to incorporate (boiling honey will break it down too much to thicken).

Step 3: Storage

Once cooled, use a funnel to pour into a glass or plastic container. Keeps very well for 2 to 3 weeks, but it starts to lose taste after that.

Green Tea Pancakes

INGREDIENTS

- 1 cup flour
- 2 Tablespoons baking powder
- 2 Tablespoons sugar
- 1 teaspoon Matcha (green tea powder)
- ⅛ teaspoon salt
- oil for skillet
- 1 ¾ cups almond milk

Optional: Slivered almonds; Earth Balance Vegan Buttery Sticks

EQUIPMENT

- mixing bowl
- electric mixer or hand whisk
- skillet

Step 1: Mix

Mix dry ingredients. Add in almond milk and mix until smooth.

 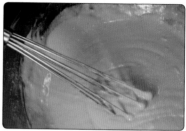

Step 2: Pour and Flip

Pour on preheated skillet. Flip when edges look dry and bubbles have formed.

Quinoa-Oat Pancakes

By Sam DeRose

http://www.instructables.com/id/Quinoa-Oat-Pancakes/

MAKES 6 TO 8 PANCAKES

One morning I was in the mood for pancakes but didn't really feel like eating some mysterious powder from a box. I came up with this recipe by randomly combining some of my favorite healthy foods, and the result turned out pretty tasty!

INGREDIENTS

- ½ cup uncooked organic quinoa
- ½ cup oats
- 2 teaspoons baking powder
- 3 egg whites
- ¾ cup unsweetened almond milk
- 1 Tablespoon chia seeds
- optional mix-ins like fruit (I added banana)
- nonstick cooking spray (I used olive oil)

Step 1: Grind and Sift

In a coffee grinder or food processor, grind up your quinoa and oats into a flour. Sift into a mixing bowl with baking powder.

Step 2: Beat and Stir

Beat the egg whites and add them and the almond milk into the dry ingredients. Stir until well combined. Stir in chia seeds. If you want, cut up some fruit into small chunks and add them into the batter.

Step 3: Pour and Flip

Heat a small nonstick pan on medium-low heat. Apply some cooking spray and add several spoonfuls of batter to the pan. Spread the batter around so it forms a 4- to 5-inch circle. Flip the pancake when the bottom begins to brown. Serve warm with sugar-free maple syrup or Greek yogurt, or just enjoy them plain!

Nutrition Facts:

Serving size:	*1 pancake (4–5 inch)*
Calories:	100
Fat:	1.7 g
Omega 3-6s:	.6 g
Sat. Fat:	.1 g
Carbs:	14.6 g
Fiber:	2.5 g
Sugar:	.8 g
Protein:	5.5 g

DRINKS AND SMOOTHIES

Banana Pecan Smoothie

By sunshiine
http://www.instructables.com/id/Banana-Pecan-Smoothie/

About five years ago one of my family members was diagnosed with Type 2 Diabetes. The doctor had mentioned that he should not drink milk. This includes ice cream and many other milk products. The contest Raw Food Recipes on Instructables.com inspired me to come up with a solution. A diabetic can eat bananas (the doctor recommended green bananas). We have a pecan tree in our yard and have plenty of pecans. This recipe is a Banana Pecan Smoothie.

INGREDIENTS

- ½ cup raw almond milk
- ½ cup raw pecan milk
- 1 green banana
- sweetener (sugar, honey, agave nectar, etc.)
- several ice cubes from filtered water
- 2 pecan halves

Note: Next time, I will cut up the banana and put it in the freezer until it is frozen.

EQUIPMENT

- blender
- glass
- spatula
- straw
- spoon (optional)

Step 1: Blend Ingredients

Put raw almond milk and pecan milk in the blender. Break up one banana and drop it in. Add sweetener according to taste. Blend well.

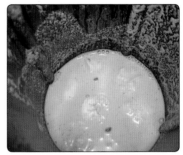

Step 2: Serve

Pour smoothie into a wine glass or regular drinking glass. Garnish with pecan halves. Serve chilled with a straw.

Mint Chocolate Chip Smoothie

By Rawfully Tempting

http://www.instructables.com/id/Mint-Chocolate-Chip-Smoothie-1/

INGREDIENTS

ALMOND MILK (SEE PAGE 2)

- ½ cup almonds, soaked overnight
- 1 ½ cups filtered water

SMOOTHIE

- 3 Tablespoons mint leaves (packed)
- 1½ frozen bananas
- 2 Tablespoons ground chia
- 2 Tablespoons hemp seed
- 2 medjool dates
- 2 drops Medicine Flower Mint Extract (optional) or ½ teaspoon mint extract
- 1 Tablespoon Love Street Chocolate Sauce (optional) or your favorite syrup
- 2 Tablespoons cacao nibs

Step 1: Make almond milk

See recipe on page 2.

Step 2: Blend

Blend almond milk with all ingredients except cacao nibs.

Step 3: Add Nibs

When mixture is creamy, add cacao nibs and pulse blend for a few seconds, leaving nibs in small chunks.

Step 4: Add Ice

Add a few ice cubes and blend again.

Pumpkin Smoothie

By annahowardshaw
http://www.instructables.com/id/Pumpkin-Smoothie/

Sitting out in the hot sun with a big slice of pumpkin pie, no matter how tempting, would seem a little out of season. But this frosty pumpkin smoothie lets you enjoy that fall treat any time of the year! Plus, flax seed, almond milk, and agave as the sweetener keep it light and low-cal.

INGREDIENTS

- 8 ounces pumpkin purée
- 1 cup unsweetened almond milk
- 3 ounces orange juice, frozen into ice cubes
- ½-inch cube of fresh ginger
- 2 Tablespoons flax seeds, ground
- 2 Tablespoons agave
- ½ teaspoon cinnamon
- 6 ounces plain Greek yogurt
- 12 ounces coconut water, frozen into ice cubes
- 2 pinches nutmeg

Step 1: Add

Add all ingredients, except ice cubes, to the blender.

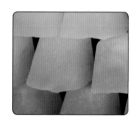

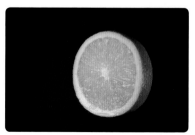

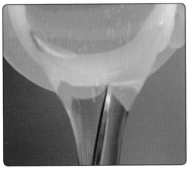

Step 2: Blend

Blend, adding a few ice cubes at a time.

Step 3: Top Off

Top with a dollop of yogurt and a dash of nutmeg.

Nutrition Facts:

Serving Size:	*1 smoothie (10 ounces)*
Calories:	111
Total Fat:	2g
Cholesterol:	0mg
Sodium:	56mg
Potassium:	293mg
Fiber:	4g
Sugars:	8g
Protein:	2g
Vitamin A:	4%
Vitamin C:	85%
Calcium:	10%
Iron:	4%

Spice Cake Special Smoothie

By shy_violet

http://www.instructables.com/id/Spice-Cake-
Special-Smoothie/

This smoothie holds a special place in my heart and is just as delicious in the summer as the winter. It also makes a fabulous base for more creative smoothies such as Carrot Cake or Zucchini Bread. Enjoy!

INGREDIENTS

- ½ frozen banana slices
- small handful of pitted dates
- 2 or 3 ice cubes
- ½ cup almond milk
- ¼–½ teaspoon chai spice (ingredients below)

CHAI SPICE

- ½ teaspoon cinnamon
- ½ teaspoon ground cloves
- ½ teaspoon ground ginger
- ½ teaspoon ground cardamom
- ¼ teaspoon black pepper

*Mix these ingredients together in a small mixing bowl and set aside.

EQUIPMENT

- blender or immersion blender
- tall chilled glass
- measuring cups and spoons
- small bowl

Step 1: Deliciousness

Add the bananas, dates, ice cubes, almond milk, and chai spice to a chilled glass

Step 2: Blend and Devour

Finally, blend all the ingredients together, sprinkle some crunchy granola on top, and drink it up!

PB & J Chocolate Bomba Smoothie

By shy_violet

http://www.instructables.com/id/PB-J-Chocolate-Bomba-Smoothie/

If you *adore* peanut butter, this is your smoothie! This is my partner's decadent morning breakfast smoothie and he would rather die than share it. So . . . I shared the recipe instead! Hope you all love it!

INGREDIENTS

- 2 heaping Tablespoons natural peanut butter
- 2 or 3 fresh strawberries, sliced
- ½ banana, sliced
- 1 scoop chocolate soy protein powder
- ½ cup almond milk
- 1 strawberry and some granola for garnish (optional)

EQUIPMENT

- chilled glass
- blender or immersion blender
- measuring spoons

Step 1: Blend

Blend all ingredients together.

Step 2: Serve

Serve in a chilled glass garnished with
a strawberry and a sprinkle of granola
for some added texture.

Dairy-Free, Chocolate-Free Hot Cocoa

By susanrm

http://www.instructables.com/id/Dairy-free-Chocolate-
free-Hot-Cocoa/

Sometimes you just want the taste of hot cocoa, but you can't (or won't) consume dairy and/or chocolate. This recipe is a pretty good substitute—warming and delicious.

INGREDIENTS

- 1 ½ Table-spoons raw carob powder
- 1 mug full of almond milk
- ½ teaspoon vanilla
- 1 teaspoon honey (optional—the carob is pretty sweet on its own)

Optional: a dash or two of cinnamon or cayenne pepper

Step 1: Mix

Simply mix all the ingredients together and stir over low heat on the stove until hot but not boiling.

Step 2: Serve

Pour into a mug and serve.

Cranberry Banana Pecan Smoothie

By sunshiine

http://www.instructables.com/id/Vegan-Cranberry-Banana-Pecan-Smoothie/

This recipe was inspired by the Raw Food Contest at Instructables.com. I must say it was challenging to make a recipe from all raw foods.

There are many health benefits from eating cranberries. They are a fruit that is high in vitamin C, which fights infections, and has been known to help with bladder infections.

INGREDIENTS

- 1 cup raw almond milk
- 1 banana
- 1 cup whole fresh cranberries
- raw organic honey

EQUIPMENT

- blender
- drinking glass
- spatula
- measuring cup
- measuring spoon

Step 1: Preparations

Place raw milk into the blender. Add the bananas and cranberries. Sweeten with honey.

Step 2: Blend

Blend for 1 minute.

Step 3: Pour and Serve

Pour into a glass. Add cranberry garnish and serve.

Vegan Nut Delight

By jennyfunbun
http://www.instructables.com/id/Vegan-Nut-Delight/

I love smoothies especially when they are truly good for me. So I am sharing my favorite good-for-me smoothie.

Using cacao powder adds a yummy chocolate taste plus fiber

INGREDIENTS

- 1 cup almond milk
- 1 banana
- ¼ cup almond meal
- 2 Tablespoons cacao powder (a good-for-you chocolate)

- 3 Tablespoons of peanut butter or other nut butter (or Nutella if you want a super chocolate experience)
- about 10 drops of chocolate stevia
- 1–2 ounces of tofu, cubed (optional for added thickness)
- 2 cups ice (optional)

and protein, without added sugars. I also use chocolate stevia as it sweetens and adds chocolate flavor but no sugars!

A lot of people use protein powders and such in their smoothies. I use tofu: it thickens the smoothie and adds protein. The almond milk, almond meal, and nut butter add flavor, thickness, and nutrition.

I also added banana because I love chocolate banana flavor!

Step 1: Almond Milk

Pour the almond milk into your blender. Use less for a thicker smoothie or more for a thinner smoothie.

Step 2: The Banana

Put the banana in your blender. You can dice it, slice it, or just toss it in!

Step 3: Nutty!

Add the almond meal, cacao powder, and peanut butter or other nut butter.

Step 4: Stevia

I then add the chocolate stevia. Using stevia means no added sugars!

Step 5: Tofu Protein

For added protein and yummy thickness, toss in the cubes of tofu.

Step 6: Add Ice and Blend

Sometimes I ice and sometimes I don't. If you choose to ice, put it in the
blender and turn it on. Blend for 3 to 4 minutes and drink your yummy
good-for-you smoothie!

Berry Banana Bash with a Kick!

By Kitty Kait

http://www.instructables.com/id/Berry-Banana-Bash-with-a-Kick/

MAKES 4 SERVINGS

This is a very healthy smoothie that tastes great. It's an easy way to get your daily vitamins. No refined sugars are added.

INGREDIENTS

- 1 cup almond milk
- ⅔ cup coconut milk
- 1 multivitamin per person, depending on the number of people drinking this batch
- 2 cups berries (if frozen then you don't need to add ice; if fresh, add ice)
- 2 bananas
- 1 shot lime syrup
- 2 Tablespoons ground flax
- 1 shot lemon juice
- ½ cup rolled oats
- ¼ cup guava nectar
- an apple, sliced

EQUIPMENT

- blender
- measuring cups
- a couple tall glasses

Step 1: Add and Blend

Add the almond milk, coconut milk, vitamins, berries, bananas, lime syrup, flax, lemon juice, oats, guava nectar, and sliced apple into the blender and blend until smooth.

Step 2: Add Ice and Enjoy

If you are using fresh berries, add half a tray of ice. Enjoy your healthy drink that is great for breakfasts.

Pumpkin Cranberry Smoothie

By savynaturalista
http://www.instructables.com/id/Pumpkin-and-Cranberry-Smoothie/

INGREDIENTS

- 1 cup pumpkin purée
- 1 cup cranberries
- 1 banana
- 1 packet stevia
- 2 cups almond milk
- ice (optional)

Step 1: Prepare

Set aside two cups and add ice.

Step 2: Blend

In a blender, blend pumpkin and cranberries; add banana and stevia. Blend until all the ingredients are incorporated.

Step 3: Add Milk

Slowly add milk to the blender and blend until the mixture becomes creamy. Add ice if desired.

Step 4: Pour and Serve

Place in cups and serve.

SNACKS, LUNCH, AND DINNER

Almond Milk

Green Tea Tortilla Chips with Fruit Salsa

By annahowardshaw

http://www.instructables.com/id/Fruit-Nachos-with-Green-Tea-Tortila-Chips/

MAKES 80 CHIPS

These lightly sweetened nacho chips are flavored with ground almonds and green tea. The fruit salsa contains lime and ginger, and the whole thing is topped with tangy Greek yogurt. A perfect summer dessert or a fun dish to share at brunch!

EQUIPMENT

- grinder
- tortilla maker (or press and skillet)
- manual or electric citrus juicer
- mixing bowls
- measuring cups/spoons
- spoon or strainer with wooden handle
- whisk or spoon
- knife or pizza cutter
- baking sheet
- paper towels
- plastic wrap
- cloth towel

INGREDIENTS

TORTILLAS

- 1½ cups flour
- ½ cup almond flour
- 1 Tablespoon green tea powder (matcha)
- 1 Tablespoon sugar
- 1 teaspoon baking powder
- 1 teaspoon canola oil
- 1 cup almond milk
- pinch of salt
- canola oil for frying
- about ¼ cup sugar to sprinkle over chips

FRUIT SALSA

- 2 cups diced mixed fruit
- 1 small container Greek yogurt
- lime juice (2 limes)
- 1 Tablespoon agave nectar
- ½ teaspoon ginger

Step 1: Tortillas

Making tortillas involves a little planning, but the process is simple and you have the ability to play around with different flavors and textures. Since I used almonds and green tea powder, neither of which is cheap, these chips come out to about the same cost as a bag of fancy-pants chips ($3.00–$4.00 per 6-ounce bag); however, you could omit the almonds (almond extract could be used instead) or flavor with something other than green tea (like cocoa powder!) to make it more economical.

To make the tortillas:

- Grind almonds (I just used a coffee grinder).
- Mix all dough ingredients together.
- If dough is still sticky, slowly add more flour just until it can be handled easily.
- Form dough into a ball, wrap it in plastic, and set aside for at least 20 minutes.
- Unwrap and knead for a couple minutes.
- Divide into 10 smaller balls.
- Cover with damp cloth for 15 minutes.
- Press each ball out in a preheated tortilla maker.
- Ideally, remove before browning begins, but a little overcooking is fine.

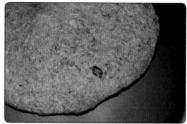

Step 2: Tortilla Chips

From tortillas to tortilla chips . . .

- Cut tortillas into eighths.
- Fry in canola oil for 1 to 2 minutes.
- Lay out on paper towels and sprinkle with sugar before they cool.

Note: Please be super careful when working with hot oil! Make sure kids, pets, or anyone on the clumsy side is away from the kitchen during this step.

Step 3: Fruit Salsa

This simple salsa adds a light citrus/ginger flavor, but does not overpower the fruit.

- Whisk together fresh lime juice, ginger, and agave.
- Pour mixture over diced fruit and stir.
- Allow to sit a few minutes before draining off excess liquid.

Step 4: Put It All Together

Spread out chips, add fruit, and top with Greek yogurt and a cherry.

Note: Assemble as close to serving time as possible as the fruit will soften the chips after a while. If you think it will be out for more than 30 minutes or so, I would recommend serving the chips in a separate dish from the fruit and yogurt to avoid this issue.

Cinnamon Swirl Sugar Quick Bread

By savynaturalista
http://www.instructables.com/id/Cinnamon-Swirl-Sugar-
Quick-Bread-Lighter-Version/

INGREDIENTS

- 2 cups all-purpose flour
- 1 teaspoon baking powder
- ½ teaspoon salt
- ¾ cup sugar
- 6 Tablespoons applesauce
- 1 egg
- 1 cup almond milk
- 1 Tablespoon cinnamon

Step 1: Preheat and Mix

Preheat oven to 350°F. In a medium bowl, mix dry ingredients and set aside.

Step 2: Beat and Add

In a large bowl, beat together ½ cup sugar, applesauce, and egg. Slowly add the flour mixture to the egg mixture alternating with the milk.

Step 3: Combine, Pour, and Sprinkle

In a small bowl, combine the cinnamon and remaining ¼ cup sugar. Pour a third of the batter into a greased loaf pan. Sprinkle a bit of the cinnamon sugar on top of batter.

Step 4: Repeat and Bake

Repeat the process twice. Bake for 45 to 60 minutes, or until a toothpick inserted in the center comes out clean. Let cool in pan.

Gluten-Free Zucchini Bread

By savynaturalista

http://www.instructables.com/id/Gluten-Free-Zucchini-Bread/

INGREDIENTS

- 1½ cup grated zucchini (packed)
- 1 cup whipped vegan butter (salted), melted
- ½ cup granulated sugar
- ½ cup brown sugar, packed
- 3 eggs
- 1 teaspoon vanilla
- ¼ cup almond milk
- 2 cups gluten-free baking mix
- ½ teaspoon baking powder
- 1 teaspoon xanthan gum
- ½ teaspoon salt

Step 1: Preheat and Shred

Preheat oven to 350°F; shred zucchini with a grater and set aside.

Step 2: Mix

In a large bowl, mix melted butter and sugar; slowly add eggs, vanilla, and milk. Mix until all the ingredients are mixed in.

Step 3: Sift and Combine

In a separate bowl, sift flour, baking powder, xanthan gum, and salt. Mix dry ingredients into the wet ingredients. Fold zucchini into mixture.

Step 4: Bake

Once done place mixture into a greased loaf pan and place in the oven. Bake bread for an hour and 10 minutes or until a toothpick stuck in the bread comes out clean. Let the bread cool before you take it out of the loaf pan.

Healthy Chocolate Banana Bread

By Sam DeRose

http://www.instructables.com/id/Healthy-Chocolate-Banana-Bread/

Bananas are literally the best fruit. They come in their own protective package, they taste great by themselves, they are the reason smoothies exist at all, and they taste amazing with chocolate, vanilla, and peanut butter (this is something that not many foods can claim).

One of my favorite foods to make with bananas is banana bread, but most recipes have oil, sugar, and chocolate as main ingredients, which are all delicious but not super healthy. So I set out on a quest to make a banana bread that I could eat for breakfast, lunch, or dinner and not feel guilty or get a stomach ache. Enjoy!

INGREDIENTS

- 2 cups quick or rolled oats
- 1 cup chocolate protein powder
- 1 cup baking Splenda or ½ cup stevia
- 1 teaspoon baking powder
- ½ cup almond milk
- ⅔ cup unsweetened apple sauce
- ⅓ cup cooked black beans
- ¼ cup chia seeds
- 2 egg whites
- 4 very ripe bananas

Optional: peanut butter, nuts, or chocolate Chips

Step 1: Mix

First, preheat your oven to 325°F. Then, mix your chia seeds and almond milk in a bowl. This is so the seeds begin to turn into a gel before you mix them in with everything else.

Step 2: Grind and Blend

Grind the oats in a blender until they are almost like flour. Dump in the rest of the dry ingredients and blend until everything is mixed. Add the wet ingredients and 3 bananas and blend for 1 to 2 minutes until thoroughly combined.

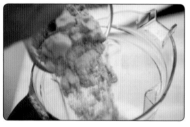

Step 3: Dice and Mix

Dice the remaining banana and mix in to the blender with a spoon. Don't turn on the blender for this step, because you will destroy your little banana chunks!

Step 4: Pour and Bake

Pour mixture into two baking pans and bake on 325°F for 1 hour or until a toothpick comes out clean.

Nutrition Facts:

Serving Size:	*1 slice (16 slices total, 8 per pan)*
Calories	120
Fat	2g
Sat Fat.	.3g
Carbs	17g
Sugar	6g
Fiber	3g
Protein	10g

Gluten-Free Strawberry Cake Bread

By savynaturalista

http://www.instructables.com/id/Gluten-Free-Strawberry-Cake-Bread/

Step 1: Preheat and Mix

Preheat oven to 375°F; in a bowl, place 2 cups of strawberries and sprinkle 2 teaspoons of sugar over them. Mix and set aside.

INGREDIENTS

- 2 cups strawberries
- 2 teaspoons sugar
- 1 cup vegan whipped butter, melted
- ½ cup brown sugar
- ½ cup white sugar
- 3 eggs
- ½ cup almond milk
- 1 teaspoon vanilla
- 2 cups gluten-free flour
- 1 teaspoon baking powder
- 1 teaspoon xanthan gum
- ½ teaspoon salt

Step 2: Mix and Add

In a large bowl use a hand mixer to mix melted butter and sugar; slowly add eggs, almond milk, and vanilla and mix until all the ingredients are mixed in.

Step 3: Sift and Combine

In a separate bowl sift flour, baking powder, xanthan gum, and salt. Mix dry ingredients into the wet ingredients. Once done, fold strawberries into the mixture.

Step 4: Bake

Place into buttered loaf pan and put in the oven. Bake bread for 60 minutes or stick a toothpick in the bread: if it comes out clean, the bread is done (the top will take a little longer).

Note: This cake bread is very moist; you could cut down on the almond milk or not use any at all. The bread is bursting with strawberries. If you do not want so many strawberries in your bread, use about a cup less.

Creamy Baked Potato Soup

By annahowardshaw

http://www.instructables.com/id/Creamy-Baked-Potato-Soup-Vegan/

Baked potato soup was one of my favorites in my pre-veggie days. This version is delicious in its own right, with or without meat and dairy substitutes.

INGREDIENTS

- 5 medium potatoes
- 6 cups veggie broth
- 2 small onions
- 3 cloves garlic
- 1 Tablespoon olive oil
- ½ cup almond milk
- 2 teaspoons salt (or to taste)
- 1 teaspoon pepper (or to taste)
- 1–2 Table-spoons of flour if needed

Note: Garnish with scallions, vegan cheese, or Smart Bacon.

EQUIPMENT

- saucepan
- cutting board
- knife
- measuring cups/spoons
- immersion blender

Step 1: Chop, Boil, Sauté

The whole thing consists of only a few quick and super-easy steps: Peel and dice potatoes, and boil potatoes in veggie broth. While potatoes are boiling, dice onions, mince garlic, and sauté both in olive oil. Once potatoes are soft, add the onions and garlic to the saucepan.

Step 2: Prep Garnishes

Chop scallions, dice "cheese," and fry "bacon."

Step 3: Blend

Break out the immersion blender and, while mixing, pour in almond milk. Add salt and pepper.

If soup is too thin, add a teaspoon of flour at a time until desired viscosity is achieved.

Step 4: Garnish

All that is left is to garnish with the fake cheese, not-really bacon, and actual scallions. If you are not big on the processed foods, this totally works without them . . . but you may want to top off with broccoli or other veggie and up the salt a bit.

Parsnip Celery Soup

By mykates3

http://www.instructables.com/id/Parsnip-Celery-Soup/

Parsnips are a fibrous root vegetable with a carrot flavor. Parsnips have a sort of spicy complexity as well as a natural sweetness; therefore, they are excellent in soup! Here is an easy recipe for parsnip celery soup topped with spicy, lemony, wilted celery leaves. It is easily made vegan and is excellent with crusty bread.

INGREDIENTS

- 2 smallish carrots
- 3 medium parsnips
- 1 potato
- small bunch of celery (save the leaves)
- 2 Tablespoons olive oil or vegan butter
- 1 onion
- 1⅞ cups almond milk
- 1⅞ cups water
- 1 dried bay leaf
- kosher salt or sea salt
- freshly ground black pepper

EQUIPMENT

- vegetable peeler
- knife
- cutting board
- large pan (a three-quart stock pan would work well)
- spoon
- blender (if you want puréed or partially puréed soup)
- 3 bowls

Step 1: Prepare the Vegetables

Peel the carrots, parsnips, and potato. Place them in a bowl filled with water to rinse off any dirt that may have accumulated during the peeling. Wash the celery.

Step 2: Prepare the Pan

Place olive oil or vegan butter into the pan. Put the pan on medium heat to preheat the pan for the vegetables.

Step 3: Prepare the Parsnips

Slice the very top and bottom off the peeled parsnips. Slice the narrow end of the parsnip into thin coins. When you reach the larger, thicker part of the parsnip, set it on the larger end, and carefully run your knife through it, cutting the vegetable in half. Lay the halves on the cutting board, and slice them in half again. Again, slice these parsnips into thin coins.

Step 4: Prepare the Carrots

Slice off the tops and bottoms of the peeled carrots, then thinly slice them into coins. If the carrots will not stay still and are rolling all over the cutting board, slice them in half.

Step 5: Prepare the Potatoes

Slice the peeled potato in half, then lay each half on the cutting board. Slice the halves into even wedges, then turn the wedges sideways and run your knife through the wedges to chop them.

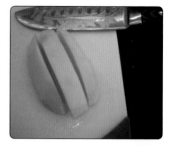

Step 6: Prepare the Onions

Slice the top and bottom off the onion, standing it on either end. Cut the onion in half, lay the two halves on the cutting board, then slice the onion halves. Turn the halves sideways and run your knife through them again to chop them. (You do not need to horizontally slice the onion in this recipe.)

Step 7: Prepare the Celery

Remove the leaves from the celery and set aside (do not throw away). Slice off the very bottom of the celery and remove anything that doesn't look right. Chop the celery.

Step 8: Add in the Vegetables

Dump all of the prepared produce into the pan.

Step 9: Cook Them

Put the lid on the pan and cook for 10 minutes. Check on the soup occasionally, giving it a stir once in a while.

Step 10: Soup Time

Add the liquids of your choosing. (Full-fat coconut milk and water work great.) Add the bay leaf.

Give the soup a big stir. Bring to a boil, then reduce the heat and simmer for 30 minutes.

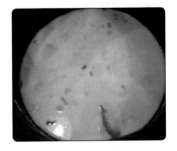

Step 11: Celery Leaves Time

Meanwhile, let us make wilted celery leaves! Here is a short overview of the recipe.

INGREDIENTS

- olive oil or other favored cooking oil
- garlic, raw or roasted
- red pepper flakes (optional)
- 1 lemon or other citrus fruit

- celery leaves
- kosher salt or sea salt
- small (1-quart) saucepan

Step 12: Wilt the Leaves!

Pour a bit of the olive oil into the pan, and set on medium heat. Chop raw or roasted garlic, and add it to the oil. Add in a pinch of red pepper flakes. The oil should be sizzling around the garlic and pepper flakes. Zest ⅓–½ of the lemon, avoiding the pith.

When the garlic and red pepper flakes have infused the oil with flavor, add in the chopped celery leaves and lemon zest. Stir, salt to taste, and turn off the heat when the leaves have reduced in size but still have crunchy bits from the stems.

Step 13: Finishing the Soup

Test your vegetables (poke with a fork to see if they are tender or eat some of them) to see if they are cooked. Once they are cooked to the desired consistency, transfer to the blender. Note: You may need to do this in batches. Also, some blenders require that food is below a certain temperature; you may want to check the manual.

Process until the soup is velvety and smooth yet retains texture from the vegetables.

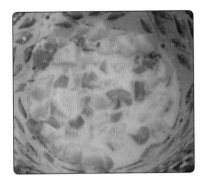 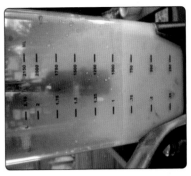

Step 14: Serve and Enjoy!

Pour the soup back into the pan it was cooked in and reheat it. Serve topped with the wilted celery leaves. This soup is great with crusty bread fresh from the oven.

Chicken Wings with Hot Sauce

By nonreactivepan

http://www.instructables.com/id/Super-Bowl-Smuper-
BowlI-Just-Want-Me-Some-Chi/

I'm a fan of sports, usually enjoy a good baseball game, and really did enjoy the World Cup while we were in Paris.

What I realize I love the most about sporting events (and everything else) are the snacks and food that go along with these events. My very favorite sports snack is the almighty chicken wing.

INGREDIENTS

FOR THE CHICKEN WINGS:

- 2 lbs chicken wings, cut into wings and drumsticks
- olive oil for roasting
- 1 egg lightly beaten
- 1 ⅓ cups almond milk
- 6 Tablespoons nondairy butter, melted
- 2 stalks of green onion, sliced thinly

FOR THE SAUCE:

- ½ cup hot sauce of your choice
- 1 cup ketchup
- ½ lemon, juiced
- 3 Tablespoons nondairy butter, softened
- 4 cloves garlic, chopped coarsely
- ½ teaspoon sesame oil
- 1 Tablespoon honey
- salt and pepper to taste

FOR THE COMBREAD:

- 1 box Gluten-Free Pantry Yankee Corn-bread mix (or
- any kind of cornbread mix you prefer)
- ¼ cup sugar

Step 1: Roast the Chicken Wings

Preheat oven to 425°F. Place the chicken wings in a roasting pan in one layer. Sprinkle with salt and olive oil. Roast for 40 minutes or until skin is browned. Remove the chicken from the oven and take it out of the pan.

Step 2: Make the Sauce

While the chicken wings are roasting, put all of the sauce ingredients in a pan and heat over low heat on the stove. You'll know it's done when it sticks to the back of a wooden spoon and it has thickened.

Step 3: Make the Cornbread

Mix all the dry ingredients in a bowl. Add the eggs, almond milk, and nondairy butter. Mix until all the dry ingredients are fully incorporated. Add the green onion. Spread the mixture evenly in a baking pan.

Step 4: Bake

Bake for 20 minutes. (It cooks in a 425°F oven, just like the chicken.) Remove, cool, and cut up into serving-sized pieces each large enough to hold a wing.

Serve It Up

Working in small batches, put a wing or two in the sauce, rolling them around to coat them thoroughly. Place a wing on top of a piece of the cornbread. Spoon a bit of sauce over the top of each wing, and add some green onions.

Roasted Butternut Squash and Pumpkin Soup

By fluffydragon

http://www.instructables.com/id/Roasted-
VegetableButternut-squashPumpkin-Soup/

MAKES 5 TO 6 SERVINGS

This is a very versatile soup—you can use different broths, vegetable or poultry, or water. You can make this vegan or vegetarian, and by default, the soup is gluten-free. You can change up the types of vegetables you want to use or leave out the pumpkin altogether. We'll start with my basic recipe.

Did I mention this recipe has only 257 calories per serving? And the cost is around $10, less if you make your own stock or broth.

EQUIPMENT

- a large soup pot
- a stick blender or regular blender
- the ability to halve a large squash without injuring oneself or the ability to purchase pre-cubed squash

INGREDIENTS

- 1 large or 2 small or medium sweet onions
- 2 red, yellow, or orange peppers, or a combo
- 1 bulb of garlic
- 1 large butternut squash
- half a bag of baby cut carrots or 3 regular carrots
- 4 Tablespoons olive oil
- 3 cups vegetable, chicken, or turkey broth, or water
- ½ can of pumpkin purée
- 1½ cups almond milk
- 2 Tablespoons cornstarch
- salt to taste
- black pepper

Optional: vegan Parmesan cheese, pumpkin seeds for garnish, black sea salt, pumpkin

Step 1: Prep Vegetables

Peel and quarter the onion(s). Wash peppers and remove stickers. Slice off the top third of the garlic bulb. Halve the squash and de-seed.

Step 2: Roast

On a baking sheet large enough to hold everything, line with foil. Place the butternut squash cut side down, and arrange the other veggies however you want, without crowding them. Wrap the garlic bulb in another piece of foil and drizzle with 1 Tablespoon of olive oil; tightly seal and place on sheet. Drizzle the remaining veggies with the rest of the olive oil. Roast at 400°F for 60 minutes, turning the peppers twice for even blackening.

Step 3: Scoop and Peel Vegetables

Turn off heat and remove from oven. Let cool for 5 to 10 minutes, then flip over the squash and scoop out the flesh into a large soup pot. Try not to get too much of the skin. Scoop up the onions and carrots and toss them in the pot. Carefully, pick a corner of pepper skin and peel it off. It should come off easily, in several large pieces. Pull off the stems, and use a fork to pick up pieces of the pepper flesh and add to pot. You shouldn't have any problem with the inner seeds. If you get some hanger-on seeds from the squash or peppers, throw them in the pot too. Don't worry about rinsing off a couple of seeds if they stick to the pepper flesh; they're edible, and you don't want to rinse off flavor.

Step 4: Add Garlic

Unwrap the garlic, hold over the pot, and squeeze gently. You should have a dozen or so roasted garlic cloves fall into the pot. Allow any leftover oil to fall in as well; and from the original baking sheet of foil, don't throw out the now flavored oil!

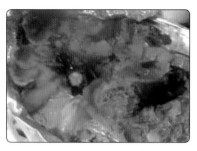

Step 5: Blend

Add your water or broth at this point, to help the blending process. If you don't have a stick blender, you can just dump everything into your regular blender and purée it. It took about a minute of stick blending to purée everything completely. Be careful, everything may still be hot at this point, so try not to splatter liquid on yourself.

Step 6: Cook

Return the purée to the pot from the blender if you used it, and put it on medium heat. Note: It was at this point that I remembered I had half a can of pumpkin purée left over from making a pumpkin pie. The purée should have nothing  in it except pumpkin. Do not use a "pumpkin pie filling" can. If you have purée and want to use it, add it at this point; about 15 ounces or one regular size—about 2 cups.

Step 7: Add Milk and Non-dairy Cheese

Add the almond milk. Add the vegan Parmesan cheese if using it; it should melt nicely. Add the cornstarch. I like it because it adds just a bit of thickness.

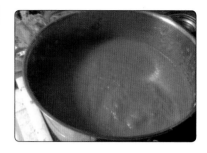

Step 8: Stir and Season

Stir to combine. My turkey broth was homemade and had no salt, so I added a teaspoon of salt to my soup. Add regular or cracked black pepper, then taste and adjust. Allow to simmer on low heat for at least 10 minutes to allow the flavors to mingle.

Step 9: Serve

Serve in large bowls garnished with grated vegan Parmesan cheese, pumpkin seeds, and/or black sea salt. If you use the canned pumpkin, this makes 5 to 6 generous servings. Otherwise, it makes around 4, but my idea of a serving isn't a dinky flat bowl, either.

Sheepish Veggie Shepherd's Pie

By annahowardshaw

http://www.instructables.com/id/Sheepish-Shepards-Pie-Veggie/

It might seem more mature to say that I made this for kids so they would find a veggie-filled meal fun, rather than just admit that this was my dinner last night!

INGREDIENTS

- 1 bulb garlic, roasted
- ½ cup vegetable broth
- 6 large potatoes
- ¾ cup almond milk
- 3 Tablespoons vegan cream cheese
- 1 Tablespoon vegan Parmesan cheese
- 4 teaspoon salt
- black food coloring
- 1 small onion, diced
- 1 cup broccoli, chopped
- 4 carrots, chopped
- 1 cup mushrooms, sliced
- 2 Tablespoons olive oil
- 3 Tablespoons red wine vinegar
- 3 ounces spinach, chopped
- 2 cups veggie crumbles*
- ½ teaspoon cumin
- 3 Tablespoons flax seed, ground
- 2 Tablespoons Herbes de Provence
- 1 teaspoon mustard powder
- 1 teaspoon pepper

*This is the only thing that keeps this from being a vegan recipe. I wanted to retain some similarity to the original. Feel free to replace with more veggies (or a vegan fake ground meat).

EQUIPMENT

- skillet
- pot to boil potatoes
- pie pan
- mixing bowls
- hand mixer
- garlic roaster
- measuring cups/spoons
- knife
- cutting board
- spatula
- cake decorator or pastry bag
- pastry tip (large star)
- pastry tip (medium circle)

Step 1: Prep Work

Before you start chopping, get your garlic roasted and veggie broth prepared. Note: There are already two great Instructables that have these covered:

Roast garlic:
www.instructables.com/id/Roasted-garlic/

Broth:
www.instructables.com/id/Vegetable-StockBullion/

Note: If you don't want to make your own veggie broth, you can buy it premade.

Step 2: Prepare Mashed Potatoes

Peel, boil, and drain potatoes. Mash with a hand mixer. Add almond milk and Tofutti cream cheese and blend. Mix in the vegan Parmesan, 1 teaspoon salt, and all the roasted garlic (perhaps less if that is not how you roll).

Step 3: Add Food Coloring

Put about ½ cup of mashed potatoes in a separate dish and stir in black food coloring. Add slowly and only use as much as you need. The color may run into the white

potatoes during baking, so using the least amount to get the effect you want will minimize this.

Step 4: Form Crust

Using a spatula, spread a thin layer of mashed potatoes along the bottom and sides of the pie pan.

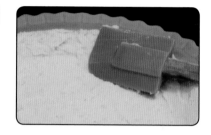

Step 5: Chop and Sauté Veggies

To prepare pie filling: Chop onion, set aside. Chop rest of veggies into vaguely even pieces. Add olive oil to a skillet and sauté onions until translucent. Add all veggies except spinach. Add red wine vinegar. Pour in broth.

Step 6: Add Seasoning

Add flax seed, mustard, cumin, Herbes de Provence, 1 Tablespoon salt and 1 teaspoon pepper.

Let cook just until colors brighten up (3 to 5 minutes or so).

Step 7: Add Spinach

Drop in spinach and veggie crumbles. Let cook until the spinach wilts (2 more minutes).

Step 8: Assemble

You are almost there! Pour all veggies into the pie crust. Note: If for some reason you don't want an adorable pie, you can simply top with the remaining mashed potatoes and bake. Otherwise . . .

Step 9: Decorate and Bake

Fill a cake decorator or pastry bag with mashed potatoes. Using a large star tip, begin outlining the body with stars. Fill in the circle, leaving the area for the head empty, except for the eyes. Switch to the dyed potato and a circle pastry tip to fill in the rest of the face, eyes, and feet.

Bake at 350°F until lightly browned, about 30 minutes.

Roasted Yellow Pepper and Roasted Tomato Soup with Hot Pepper Cream

By craftyweetzie

http://www.instructables.com/id/Roasted-Yellow-Pepper-Soup-and-Roasted-Tomato-Soup/

This is a delicious soup, especially for fall! Actually, it's two soups mixed into one, sweet and roasted, with a bit of sweet heat to kick it up a notch.

INGREDIENTS

YELLOW PEPPER SOUP:

- 6 yellow bell peppers, roasted and coarsely chopped (about 6 cups)
- 3 Tablespoons finely chopped shallot
- 1 teaspoon fresh thyme, chopped
- 1 Tablespoon vegan margarine (I use Earth Balance)
- 1½ cups vegan bouillon plus additional to thin the soup as needed (I use Rapunzel with sea salt.)
- ¼ cup unsweetened almond milk
- fresh lemon juice to taste

TOMATO SOUP:

- 3 pounds tomatoes, quartered
- 3 unpeeled large garlic cloves
- 3 Tablespoons finely chopped shallot
- ½ teaspoon dried oregano, crumbled
- 1 Tablespoon vegan margarine
- 1½ cups vegan bouillon plus additional to thin the soup as needed (I use Rapunzel with sea salt.)
- ¼ cup unsweetened almond milk
- fresh lemon juice to taste

HOT PEPPER CREAM:

- 3 fresh hot cherry peppers, blackened over an open flame and chopped fine (wear rubber gloves)
- 1 large garlic clove, minced and mashed to a paste
- ½ cup vegan sour cream

Yellow Pepper Soup:

Step 1: Char or Broil

Char the peppers over an open flame or broil them in an oven to roast.

Step 2: Cook and Simmer

In a large saucier, cook the shallot, thyme, vegan margarine, and salt and pepper to taste over medium-low heat, stirring, until the shallot is soft and translucent. Add the bell peppers and vegan bouillon, and simmer the mixture, covered, until the peppers are very soft (about 15 minutes).

Step 3: Purée

In a blender, purée the soup in batches until it is very smooth. Pour back into the pan and whisk in the almond milk, additional broth until it's a consistency you like, the lemon juice, and salt and pepper to taste.

Tomato Soup:

Step 4: Bake

Spread the tomatoes in one layer, skin side down, in 2 foil-lined jelly-roll pans, add the garlic to 1 of the pans, and bake the tomatoes and the garlic in a preheated 350°F oven for 45 minutes to 1 hour, or until the tomatoes are very soft and their skin is dark brown. Let the tomatoes and the garlic cool in the pans on racks.

Step 5: Cook and Simmer

In a heavy saucepan, cook the shallot, oregano, vegan margarine, and salt and pepper to taste over medium-low heat, stirring, until the shallot is soft. Add the tomatoes, the garlic (skins discarded), and vegan bouillon, and simmer the mixture, covered, for 15 minutes.

Step 6: Purée

In a blender purée the soup in batches until it is very smooth, forcing it as it is puréed through a fine sieve set over the pan, cleaned, and whisk in the almond milk, additional broth if necessary (both soups should have the same consistency), lemon juice, and salt and pepper to taste.

Note: The soup may be made 1 day in advance, kept covered and chilled, and reheated.

Hot Pepper Cream:

Step 7: Blend

Blend together the chilies, garlic, and vegan sour cream until smooth.

Step 8: Serve and Eat!

To serve the soup: Take ½ cup of each soup and pour them simultaneously into a shallow soup bowl from opposite sides of the bowl. Drizzle about ½ Tablespoon of the sour cream mixture on the top.

Tender Seitan Slices in Herbed Gravy

By SLCVeganista

http://www.instructables.com/id/Tender-Seitan-Slices-In-Herbed-Gravy/

As a longtime dedicated vegan, I am always looking for main-course alternatives to meat, poultry, and fish.

Seitan (pronounced say-tahn) is not to be confused with Satan, which is also known as the Devil. Seitan isn't evil; it's just misunderstood.

Seitan has been around for centuries, but for the average consumer, it seems it is only now a new revelation. Seitan is also known as Meat of Wheat, as it is made using vital wheat gluten.

Making your own seitan isn't as complicated as most people assume it is. It can take a long time, if you make it completely from scratch (which involves isolating the wheat gluten on your own by starting with 8 cups of white flour and 8 cups of whole wheat flour mixed with water to form a dough, and then washing and rinsing the dough until all the water runs clear, which can take several hours).

Over the years, I have tried many, many seitan recipes and all of them fell short somehow, so I developed this recipe using a lot of trial and error. I think it has reached Perfection as well as an award-winning status.

Lucky for all of you, there are shortcuts that make this very easy to make! The key to this recipe is the gravy. If your gravy is good, your seitan will also taste good. We all like easy and uncomplicated recipes, especially during the hectic holiday season when time always runs out at the most inopportune moments.

INGREDIENTS
HERBED GRAVY

- ¼ cup vegan margarine (I use Earth Balance Original, either Buttery Spread or Buttery Sticks.)
- ½ cup fresh minced herbs of choice (rosemary, oregano, thyme, sage, etc.)
- 2 Tablespoons dried herbs of choice (usually a mixture of Organic Poultry Seasoning and Kirkland Organic No Salt Seasoning from Costco)
- ¼ cup tapioca flour (Bob's Red Mill or other brand)
- 4 cups plain unsweetened almond milk
- 2 vegan chicken-style bouillon cubes (I use No-Chicken Bouillon Cubes from Edward & Sons.)
- 1–2 teaspoons garlic granules or powder
- 1–2 teaspoons onion powder or flakes
- salt and pepper, to taste

SEITAN

- 1 15-ounce can organic garbanzo beans, drained and rinsed (or dried garbanzo beans that have been fully cooked, drained and rinsed)
- 3 cups vital wheat gluten flour (I use Bob's Red Mill, but use whatever you can find.)
- 2 cups Herbed Gravy

Note:
Bouillon cubes are salty, so you probably won't need to add any additional salt)

EQUIPMENT

- heavy duty aluminum foil
- food processor with an S-blade
- steamer (You can use a big pot with a lid and a colander instead if that is all you have.)
- colander
- measuring cups
- can opener (if you are using canned garbanzo beans)
- saucepan
- spoon or spatula for stirring

Step 1: Make Gravy

You will want to make the gravy first. Melt margarine/heat oil in a saucepan on low heat. Add minced herbs. Dissolve cornstarch/tapioca starch/flour in 3 cups cold, plain, unsweetened almond milk. Add to saucepan, along with vegan bouillon cube dissolved in water, garlic, onion powder, and salt and pepper, if desired. Stir continuously on medium heat until gravy thickens.

Step 2: Cool

Once made, set it aside and allow to cool. (It can be warm, but if it is too hot, you will burn your hands when trying to knead the seitan.)

Step 3: Set Up Processor and Prep Beans

Set up your food processor with the S-blade. Prepare garbanzo beans by draining and rinsing off with cool water in a colander. Add garbanzo beans to the food processor bowl and pulse for 30 to 45 seconds, or until they are well chopped (but not puréed).

Step 4: Add Gravy and Flour

Add cooled gravy to pulsed garbanzo beans. Pulse again for 30 to 45 seconds or until well blended. Slowly add vital wheat gluten flour to the food processor a cup at a time. You know when it's done when it starts to form a ball of soft, stretchy, slightly shiny dough.

Step 5: Knead and Roll Out

Remove from food processor and knead for 3 to 5 minutes or until smoothed out. Cover and allow to rest 30 minutes. Meanwhile, start a pot of water to boil or set up a steamer. Break into 4 smaller balls of dough and roll out into logs.

Step 6: Steam

Wrap tightly in foil and steam seitan for 1 hour and 15 minutes. Depending on your steamer size, you may not be able to fit all of them in there at once. That's OK, but make sure all your raw seitan is wrapped in foil until ready to be steamed. It is best to steam it as soon as possible though, because it doesn't turn out as well if you wait more than a couple of hours to steam it.

Step 7: Cool, Slice, Bake

Carefully remove foil packet from steam, unwrap and allow to cool slightly before slicing.

After being steamed and sliced, place slices in a lightly greased baking dish, completely cover slices with Herbed Gravy, then cover dish with foil and bake at 350°F for 60 to 90 minutes.

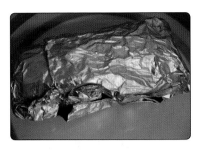

Step 8: Serve

Serve alongside other veganized Thanksgiving foods (such as mashed potatoes, festive cranberry relish, candied yams, wild rice stuffing, and, if you are not stuffed, gluten-free vegan pumpkin or pecan pie!

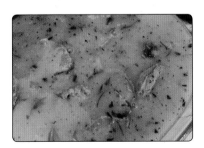

Ghoul-icious Sausage and Pumpkin Soup

By MaryT8M

http://www.instructables.com/id/Ghoul-icious-Sausage-And-Pumpkin-SoupIts-Spoo/

A friend of mine gave me this recipe many years ago. I think she got it off the Internet on a low–carb recipe site. I've seen it floating around since then. It has been our go-to recipe every Halloween as well as any time we want an easy-to-make, great tasting soup.

This is *not* low fat as written, but *is* low carb. You could do a few adjustments to lower the fat/calorie count. I'll list some of the changes I've made.

INGREDIENTS

- 1 pound tube of hot sausage (You can use regular or lower fat sausage, and you could add red pepper flakes if you can't find hot.)
- 1 medium onion, chopped
- 1–2 cloves of garlic, chopped (I have used garlic from a jar also.)
- 1 rounded Tablespoon of Italian (or spaghetti) spices
- 8 ounces of fresh mushrooms, sliced (You can use canned sliced mushrooms.)
- 15-ounce can of pumpkin purée (*not* pumpkin pie filling)
- 4 cups chicken broth (I used 2 cans of chicken broth.)
- 1 cup almond milk

EQUIPMENT

- large saucepan
- knife
- cutting board
- measuring spoons and cups
- can opener

Step 1: Brown and Chop

Brown the sausage in the large saucepan . . . there is no need to brown it in a skillet; this will save you from washing an extra pan. Chop the onion while the sausage is browning.

Step 2: Drain

Drain the sausage and return it to the pan.

Step 3: Add and Sauté

Once the sausage is back in the pan, add chopped onion, chopped garlic, Italian spice (or spaghetti spice), and mushrooms. Sauté until the sausage is cooked and the onions are translucent.

Step 4: Add and Simmer

Add the can of pumpkin and mix *well*. Stir in the broth and simmer 20 minutes, stirring once or twice.

Step 5: Finish

Stir in almond milk and simmer for another 10 minutes (*do not* let it boil). Salt and pepper to taste (I never add any).

Step 6: Serve and Enjoy

I know this sounds like an odd combination, but it's really great. I've never had anyone not like it, and I've shared this recipe over and over. This is a filling, hearty, healthy soup.

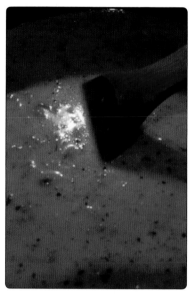

Vegan Cream of Potato Soup with Mushrooms

By joe

http://www.instructables.com/id/Vegan-Cream-of-Potato-Soup-w-mushrooms./

A tasty cold weather treat, which can be made vegan or vegetarian.

INGREDIENTS

- 5–6 potatoes, cubed
- 1 onion, diced
- 4 ounces mushrooms, quartered
- 2 cloves garlic, minced
- 5 Tablespoons vegan butter
- 3 cups almond milk
- 3 cups veggie broth (I use Knorr veggie bouillon to make this.)
- 4 Tablespoons flour
- fresh ground pepper, to taste
- Jane's Krazy Mixed Up Salt, to taste

Step 1: Cook and Prep

Cube potatoes and boil. While that's going on, dice the onion, cut the mushrooms into quarters, and mince the garlic.

Step 2: Cook and Drain

Drain the potatoes when they are done (should take about 15 minutes). Cook the onions, garlic, mushrooms, and butter together in a big saucepan for 5 minutes.

Step 3: Add, Season, and Serve

Stir in the almond milk, veggie broth, potatoes, and flour. Simmer for 10 minutes. Season and serve!

DESSERT

Chocolate Avocado Mousse

By jessyratfink
http://www.instructables.com/id/Chocolate-avocado-mousse/

This is something I've been seeing all over the Internet—chocolate avocado mousse! Sounds crazy, I know. But it works. It's actually super tasty! I think I'll be getting my creamy chocolate fix this way from now on. It is also a really excellent vegan dessert you can throw together in no time.

INGREDIENTS

- 1 large avocado
- ¼ cup cocoa powder
- ¼ cup almond milk
- ¼ cup honey
- 1 teaspoon vanilla

Using the amounts above, you end up with a dark-chocolate-style mousse. Not too sweet! If you'd like a more milk-chocolate flavor, I suggest using a little less cocoa powder and more honey.

Step 1: Combine

Put everything into a food processor or blender. Break the avocado up into smaller pieces to make it easier on your machine.

Step 2: Blend

Process for 10 to 15 seconds and then stop and scrape down the sides. Then process again until nice and smooth.

You can eat it right away or chill for a little while before you dig in. I just wouldn't let it sit too long in the fridge—once the avocado starts oxidizing it will alter the flavor—and not in a good way!

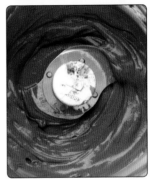

Easy Chocolate Chip Cookies That Happen to Be Vegan

By Domineke
http://www.instructables.com/id/Chocolate-Chip-Cookies-that-Just-Happen-to-be-Vega/

MAKES 2 DOZEN COOKIES

For a class party, a vegan friend brought freshly baked chocolate chip cookies. Once only gooey crumbs were left, she told the class they were vegan. People looked shocked to find out that vegan cookies could be so delicious. And, when I asked her for the recipe, I found out they were also super easy to make with "normal" ingredients. You won't have to hunt through specialty stores for obscure ingredients while your stomach is begging for cookies. So even if you are baking-challenged, and have only a few ingredients in your cupboard, you can easily have a bellyful of cookies in about half an hour. Or, because this recipe does not use eggs, you could have a bellyful of cookie dough in even less time!

INGREDIENTS

- 2 cups unbleached flour
- 2 teaspoons baking powder
- ½ teaspoon salt
- ¾ cup of vegan chocolate chips
- 1 teaspoon cinnamon (optional)
- ¾ cup raw sugar
- ½ cup canola or vegetable oil or vegan margarine (depending on your preference)
- 1 teaspoon vanilla extract
- ½ cup almond milk

EQUIPMENT

- large bowl
- medium bowl
- measuring cup
- measuring spoons
- whisk or silicon spatula (for mixing)
- baking sheets
- oven mitt

I used semisweet chocolate chips. Many semisweet and dark chocolate chips in baking aisles are vegan. Just make sure to check the ingredients because many popular baking chips do have milk fat. You could also use carob chips, but I know fewer people prefer those to semisweet or dark chocolate chips. You could also skip the chips. I actually prefer chipless cookies and know that these cookies are also delicious without the chips!

Bake time: 9–15 minutes, which will vary depending on your oven. My oven takes 12 minutes to bake these cookies.

I use a silicon spatula because it mixes the liquid ingredients and dry ingredients even better than a whisk with this particular recipe. If you only have a whisk, that is fine, but the dough might get caught and you will have to constantly pick it out. If you only have a whisk, I would recommend using your hands.

Read before starting:
- Do not grease the baking sheet. There is enough oil in the batter.
- It is ideal that the ingredients are room temperature for baking, but it's not necessary.
- Do not put the cookie sheets on the stove while the oven is hot. This will cause the sheets to heat, and the cookies will bake unevenly.
- These cookies do not spread much while baking, so feel free to place them close together on the baking sheet.
- Do not leave them in too long. These cookies will come out soft, but they will harden when they cool. Because they come out soft, a friend told me she accidentally burned them.
- Lastly, always remember to have your oven mitt handy.

 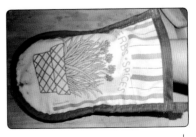

Step 1: Preheat and Mix the Dry

Preheat oven to 350°F. In a large bowl, mix flour, baking powder, salt, chocolate chips, and cinnamon. Make a well in the center of the dry ingredients and set the bowl aside.

Why make this hole in the middle? Later, you will be pouring the wet ingredients into this hole. Digging the hole in the middle of the ingredients will make enveloping the wet ingredients with the dry ingredients much easier.

Step 2: Mix Wet Ingredients with Sugar

In a medium-sized bowl, mix raw sugar, canola or vegetable oil or vegan margarine, vanilla extract, and almond milk.

Note: If you want your cookies more cakelike, add a little bit more liquid (i.e., more almond milk).

Step 3: Pour Wet into Dry

Pour the wet ingredients into the hole you made earlier in the dry ingredient's bowl. Mix it well, but do not overwork the dough. Not overworking the dough means it will not get too thin. Remember to scrape the bottom of the bowl for dry ingredients you might miss.

Step 4: Spoon Dough onto Baking Sheets

Spoon dough onto ungreased cookie sheets in Tablespoon-sized scoops.

Step 5: Put Baking Sheets in Oven

Put cookie sheets in the oven vertically.

Step 6: Rotate Sheets 180 Degrees

After baking for 5 minutes, rotate the baking sheets 180 degrees so that they are in the oven horizontally. Let them bake for another 4 minutes. If they look done, take them out. If they do not look done, check the cookies every 2 minutes until they are to your liking. Again, the cookies are done when they seem a little bit softer than you would want them to be. They will significantly harden once as they're cooling.

Step 7: Take Them out of Oven

Once the cookies are done baking, take the sheets out, one at a time, using your oven mitts. Set the sheets on a stable counter. Move the cookies onto wire cooling racks with a spatula. If you do not have a wire cooling rack, you can use wooden cutting boards. I decided to use wooden cutting boards because wood is not a good conductor of heat. The method has worked just fine.

Note: If the cookies start to crumble when you to begin to transfer them to the cooling rack or wooden cutting board, let them sit on the sheet for 2 more minutes.

Step 8: Enjoy!

Lastly, make sure you get someone to wash the dishes, because you'll be busy eating the cruelty-free sweets of your labor.

Banana "Ice Cream"

By sisssy17

http://www.instructables.com/id/Banana-Ice-cream-
Vegan-Healthy/

This is one of my favorite summer treats! It's healthy, easy to make, and most important— *delicious*!

Step 1: Prep

Line a baking sheet with foil or wax paper.

Step 2: Peel and Slice

Take a banana, peel it, and slice it completely onto the baking sheet. Slices should be about ¼ to ½ inch thick. (Not too thick and not too thin). Make sure the pieces are laying flat and not overlapping (this will help them freeze quicker and more evenly). I use one medium–large banana as a one-person serving size. One banana will make about 1 cup of "ice cream."

INGREDIENTS
- Bananas
- Almond milk

Optional:
- Shredded coconut
- Dark chocolate
- Chopped nuts
- Flax seeds
- Honey
- Peanut butter
- Ice cream toppings

EQUIPMENT
- food processor or blender (I use a Nutribullet.)
- knife
- wax paper or aluminum foil
- baking sheet
- freezer

Step 3: Freeze

Put the baking sheet into the freezer and allow the bananas to freeze for at least 3 hours. You want them to be really frozen when you are blending them. I usually cut up a couple of bananas at the beginning of the week and keep them frozen for at least a day before making this.

Step 4: Blend

When your bananas are frozen, peel them off the wax paper or them into the food processor. For each banana (if one banana = 20 slices, then I mean for each 20 slices), put ¼ cup almond milk. Start with this, and if you have too much difficulty blending add more, but you want as little milk as possible to keep your ice cream cold and creamy! (If you want to add flax seeds, peanut butter, or anything else you can add it at the beginning before you start blending or after you've blended for a bit; try not to wait until the very end so you don't have to overblend your ice cream.)

Step 5: Pulse

Pulse your food processor, blender, or Nutribullet to blend your bananas. This can be really frustrating, especially if you are hungry for some delicious ice cream; be patient and readjust your bananas as much as needed until you get them to blend to the right consistency. If it takes you more than a couple of minutes to blend your bananas, you can add almond milk, one Tablespoon at a time, to your mixture.

Make sure you don't overblend. Once you have all the banana chunks out of your mixture, the consistency should be exactly that of soft-serve ice cream!

Step 6: Top and Serve

Scoop into a bowl, add toppings and enjoy!

Note: When I'm making this I like to use ground flax seeds and top with shredded coconut and chopped nuts. It is also very good with dark chocolate and peanut butter! I like using very ripe bananas to make this because I like the taste, but the less ripe your bananas are when you freeze them, the less banana-like your ice cream will taste. If you overblend, you can simply stick your bowl in the freezer for a while. This is one of my favorite treats, a much healthier version of ice cream and tastes delicious.

Healthier Cupcakes with Granola and Strawberry

By Sherrybaby81485

http://www.instructables.com/id/Healthier-Cupcakes-Granola-Strawberry/

With my new healthy goal of eating right I have stopped buying junk food. So when it was time for the Sunday potluck I wasn't sure what to bring. I didn't have the ingredients to make my cute sugary-frosting creation cupcakes, but I did have plenty of strawberries and granola! It's pos-sible to make healthier desserts that still taste good!

INGREDIENTS

- 2 cups whole wheat flour
- ½ teaspoon salt
- 2 teaspoons baking powder
- ¾ cup brown sugar
- 1 cup vegetable oil
- 1 egg
- ½ cup almond milk
- 1 cup granola + extra for garnish, chopped
- 1 cup strawberries, chopped

FROSTING

- 1 container fat-free vegan cool whip
- 1 package sugar-free, fat-free vegan vanilla pudding
- 1 cup vanilla almond milk
- 1 cup strawberries sliced

Step 1: Preheat and Prepare

Preheat oven to 350°F. Prepare cupcake pan with papers. In a large mixing bowl, combine the dry ingredients and whisk to mix well.

Step 2: Mix Dry and Wet

Mix liquid ingredients into dry ingredients and stir. Fold in the 1 cup of granola and strawberries.

 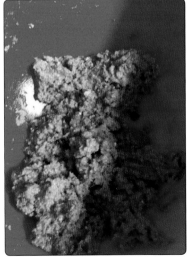

Step 3: Fill and Bake

Fill cupcake pan with full scoop of batter into each cup. Sprinkle with remaining granola. Bake for 20–25 minutes until muffin springs back or a knife is inserted and comes out clean.

Step 4: Make Frosting

Once cooled, make frosting. In a medium bowl, combine pudding mix with milk. Mix until smooth. Gently fold in whipped topping until no streaks remain. Spread evenly over cupcakes. Then top with sliced strawberries.

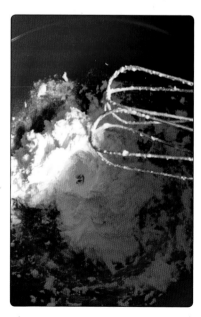 

Raw Chocolate Almond Chia Pudding

By annahowardshaw

http://www.instructables.com/id/Raw-Chocolate-Almond-Chia-Pudding/

Chia seeds are not just for growing on novelty clay pots . . . apparently they are very good for you. This is pretty much the simplest chia pudding possible, and several versions of it can be found quickly online. It is also a fast and easy raw food recipe which doesn't require much advance planning. The consistency is somewhere between Jell-O and tapioca and makes a great breakfast, snack, or dessert.

INGREDIENTS

- 2 cups almond milk
- ½ cup chia seeds (whole or ground)
- 3 Tablespoons raw cacao powder
- 2 Tablespoons agave

Optional additions: Berries, banana, cinnamon, cocoa nibs, or anything else you can think of!

Step 1: Mix and Whisk

Put all ingredients in a mixing bowl, whisk thoroughly, and let sit for at least 20 minutes. Seriously, that's it.

Mochi Cupcakes

By purelily
http://www.instructables.com/id/Mochi-Cupcakes-Gluten-
Free-Versatile-and-Healthy-i/

If you love mochi and other chewy, dense desserts, then you have to try these cupcakes! They're naturally gluten-free and super versatile, as you can see in the various toppings I used in this batch (though the plain version is just as delicious). I've also made some substitutions for the typically copious amounts of butter in mochi and cut the sugar so that these are just sweet enough.

INGREDIENTS

- 2 Tablespoons vegan butter, softened (in the sun in my case)
- ½ cup sugar
- 2 Tablespoons "sun-butter" or almond butter
- ⅓ cup mashed banana (about ¾ of a small banana)
- ¾ cup almond milk

- 2 eggs
- 1 teaspoon vanilla extract
- 1 teaspoon baking powder
- 1 teaspoon cinnamon
- ½ teaspoon ground ginger
- ⅛ teaspoon salt
- 1¼ cups glutinous rice flour (a.k.a mochiko or sweet rice flour)

OPTIONAL TOPPINGS:

- Chocolate chips
- shredded coconut

- nuts or seeds
- cacao nibs

Note: Some shoppers will only buy the Blue Star Mochiko rice flour, but I have had an easier time finding the Thai version and have had no problems with it in my baking. So feel free to use whatever you can get your hands on—just make sure it's not regular rice flour.

Step 1: Soften Butter

Cut butter into small blocks and place in a large mixing bowl in the sun for about 2 minutes to soften. (If you're baking on a cloudy day or at night, you can stick it in a zipped plastic baggie and immerse it in warm water for 3 minutes.)

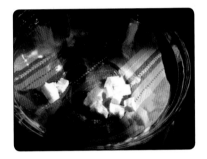

Step 2: Mix

Add the sugar, sun-butter, and banana in with the vegan butter and start mashing and mixing. (I had some leftover cinnamon sugar, so I used that instead; but don't worry, you'll be adding cinnamon in later!) Try to get all the large lumps of banana out, but it doesn't have to be perfect.

Step 3: Add and Mix

Add the next 3 ingredients in the list to the mixing bowl—milk, eggs, and vanilla extract—and mix well. Then mix in the next 4 ingredients: baking powder, cinnamon, ginger, and salt.

Remember, no lumps! No one likes a bite of pure baking powder.

Step 4: Slowly Add Rice Flour

Now add the glutinous rice flour to the bowl in small batches and fully mix it in before adding more. Your end batter should be slightly thick.

Step 5: Preheat and Prep

Preheat the oven to 350°F. Line your muffin tin with either silicone baking cups and/or some good nonstick paper cups. I used a combination because I ran out of the silicone ones. (They both worked great at not sticking to the cupcakes, but the silicone ones had a better shape.)

Divide the batter evenly among the 12 cups.

Note: You could probably bake this in a 9x13 pan and just cut it into bars, but I'm not sure how long you would bake it for, so just keep an eye on it if you try it that way.

Step 6: Add Toppings (optional)

Here's the fun part . . . sprinkle on your toppings! As I mentioned earlier, the plain mochi is also really yummy, but life is so much more fun with toppings! I used pecans, cacao nibs, dried blueberries, chocolate chips, and unsweetened, medium-shred coconut flakes. The chocolate coconut was my favorite.

Step 7: Bake and Cool

Pop the muffin tin into the oven for 25 to 30 minutes depending on your oven. You'll see the cupcakes rise a bit, and when a toothpick comes out fairly clean, they are done. Carefully transfer them to a cooling

rack, where they will deflate a little. Give them about 10 minutes to cool (or not!), and then dive into the ooey, gooey, sticky, chewy goodness!

Storage Tips:

Once cooled, I store them in the fridge because I am just not sure about keeping anything with egg in it at room temperature. These also freeze beautifully. I put a few in the freezer and I move one to the fridge a few hours before I am ready to eat it. I haven't tried eating it partially frozen yet, but maybe that would be a nice texture!

Raw Vegan Mango Pie

By susanrm

http://www.instructables.com/id/Raw-Vegan-Mango-Pie/

Raw vegans find creative ways to eat food that resembles the foods they love, but which is not subjected to the high heat that kills many of the nutrients in live food.

I am not a raw vegan, but I have tried it out, and I have friends who are. Regardless, this pie is delicious. One family brought something similar to my K-1 class for a birthday party, and all the children loved and devoured it. That tells you something!

My additional challenge was to make it only with things I had in my cupboard. This worked except for the mangos, as I had this idea after having eaten my last mango.

Obviously, this recipe is not safe for those allergic to nuts.

INGREDIENTS

CRUST:

- ½ cup almonds
- 1 cup walnuts
- maple syrup or agave

FILLING:

- 1 mango
- 1 medium banana
- juice of half of a lemon
- ⅛ cup shredded coconut
- ⅛ cup almond milk
- ¼ cup blueberries (can be frozen)
- raspberries (optional)
- maple syrup or agave

Step 1: Make the Crust

Using a food processor or appropriate blender with a chopping attachment, chop the nuts finely but well before nut-butter stage. Mix in 3 to 4 teaspoons of maple syrup until the mixture sticks together. Press the crust into the pie plate. It doesn't have to go all the way up the sides.

Step 2: Make the Filling

Peel the mango with a vegetable peeler, then cut the fruit away from the pit. In your blender, blend the mango fruit. Add banana, lemon juice, coconut, almond milk, 1 teaspoon maple syrup, and blueberries. Blend well until smooth.

Step 3: Pour into Crust

Pour mixture into the pie crust. Garnish with raspberries if you wish. My berries were wild ones I picked last summer, which I thought was a nice DIY touch.

Step 4: Serve

Serve right away, or refrigerate, or freeze for an ice cream–like treat. Enjoy your pie!

 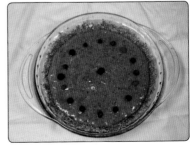

Vegan Pumpkin Pie

By scoochmaroo

http://www.instructables.com/id/Vegan-Pumpkin-Pie/

It is important to make this pie the day before serving so that it has a chance to set really well.

My main complaint about this recipe is that it uses one and a half cans of pumpkin purée, so it really works better if you make two at once—or, preferably, use fresh pumpkin!

INGREDIENTS

PIE CRUST:

- 1¼ cups all-purpose flour
- ⅓ cup nonhydrogenated vegetable shortening
- 3 Tablespoons cold water

PIE FILLING:

- 2 cups solid-pack canned pumpkin (If you use home-cooked pumpkin, drain it for several hours hanging in a cloth bag, so it's thick like canned pumpkin.)
- 1 cup almond milk
- ¾ cup brown sugar or Sucanat
- ¼ cup cornstarch
- 1 Tablespoon molasses or blackstrap molasses
- 1 teaspoon ground cinnamon
- 1 teaspoon vanilla
- ½ teaspoon of each: ground ginger, nutmeg, and salt
- ¼ teaspoon ground allspice or cloves
- tofu or flour, as much as is desired for filling consistency (optional)

Step 1: Make the Crust

Preheat oven to 350°F. Using a food processor, pulse together flour and shortening until mixture resembles coarse pea-sized crumbs. Add water 1 Tablespoon at a time, pulsing after each addition, until dough creates one mass. Roll out dough on lightly floured surface and place in pie plate. Do not pierce crust with fork.

Step 2: Make the Filling

In a food processor, combine all filling ingredients and process until smooth.

Step 3: Bake

Bake for 60 minutes, turning halfway through. Cover the edges of the crust with foil if they start to brown too much. Let cool and refrigerate overnight before serving.

Note: After tasting the final pie, I decided on adding tofu or flour into the filling, as the finished result was very similar to eating a can of pumpkin purée with no real body to it!

Enjoy!

Almond Dessert Threesome

By supersoftdrink
http://www.instructables.com/id/Almond-Threesome/

Some late mornings just beg an indulgent dish to echo an indulgent previous evening . . . especially if your companions from the indulgent evening are still with you at brunch.

I wanted to make an artistic dessert-y dish that was still light enough to be served with brunch. I love the almond and its many incantations, and decided to showcase three different presentations. I wanted a lot of contrast in the dish; I chose a soft but dense, buttery almond cake and a light, sweet, crisp macaron to accompany the mild, creamy, and soft gelled panna cotta.

Macarons are simple if the planets and stars align and everything goes perfectly. The other 99.99 percent of the time, they're a pain. I used this recipe for the macarons because it has volume measurements and I can't find part of my digital kitchen scale.

The recipes I found were just too dry for my taste, and I was really tired of separating eggs by then. I remembered the texture of the layers of Italian ribbon cookies I made a couple of holidays ago and decided to adapt that recipe for this dish.

My sister Kripa doesn't like the taste of most almond things. She says they taste too sharp. I suspect she's referring to heavy use of almond extract, so I wanted to make something she'd find palatable. Most almond panna cotta I've seen uses a fair amount of almond extract, and I wanted to emphasize the creamy nuttiness of the almond. Commercial almond milk was a bit too thin and watery, and I didn't want the almond milk to be overpowered by the cream, so I made my own with more almond. That way, I was able to use whole milk instead of cream to make a lighter but not too light panna cotta.

I love cherries with almond, but they're not in season now and I couldn't even find second-rate ones at the store. I compromised by using cherry juice as one component and two other fresh fruits for the dish. I also used three varieties of chocolate (dark, milk, and white) to continue the threesome theme.

I played around with two platings for this dish; one includes the tart cherry tapioca pearls and the strawberry milk chocolate sauce; the other does not. (Yes, I know the spoon is on the wrong side. I was in a hurry!)

This recipe makes four plates, but there will be extra macarons. That shouldn't be a problem for most people.

Almond Macarons

There are many food blogs with huge sections devoted to the trial and error of macarons. Lots of them suggest letting the egg whites sit out overnight to thicken. I guess less water in the batter makes better macarons. I didn't want to leave raw egg sitting out for hours and then serve a dish made with said eggs. Instead, I used smaller egg whites (less water) and added a little bit of powdered egg whites. I don't have a Silpat and I ran out of parchment, so I used nonstick aluminum foil. It worked just fine.

Some recipes also say to leave the pan of piped macaron batter out for an hour or so to form a skin before baking. But I didn't want to wait.

INGREDIENTS

- 1 cup almond meal
- 1 ¼ cups powdered sugar
- ¼ cup egg whites
- ½ teaspoon powdered egg whites
- 1 pinch salt
- ¼ cup white sugar

Step 1: Preheat and Prep

Preheat the oven to 300°F and line a pan or two with something nonstick.

Step 2: Sift and Mix

Sift the almond meal together with the powdered sugar. Mix the egg whites with the powdered egg white; this will take some time for the powder to hydrate and get rid of the little lumps. Don't beat the egg whites right now; just mix them until the lumps are gone.

Step 3: Whip

Add the salt, then whip until they start to get foamy. You want to gently unravel the egg proteins here, not beat them into submission just yet. When the egg whites start to get foamy, slowly add the white sugar while still whipping. You can increase the speed now. Whip the egg whites until they just barely form stiff peaks, but don't overwhip or they'll tighten and get lumpy.

Step 4: Fold and Stir

Gently fold in the almond meal mixture, half at a time. Don't stir too hard and do *not* overstir, or you'll deflate the egg whites and the batter will be too runny. Because I'm still a bit of a noob [newbie]

in the kitchen, I made sure to fold until things were *almost* mixed, but not quite. That way, when I scooped it into the bag and piped it, it wouldn't get overmixed. Notice in the pictures that the batter seems stiff at first, but then spreads out on the pan. You don't want it to be runny right away.

Step 5: Scoop and Pipe

Scoop the batter into a large ziplock bag, snip off a corner, and pipe into little mounds on the prepared pan. Whack the pan on the stove if you think it'll help remove air bubbles, or leave it to sit for an hour or so if you think that might help.

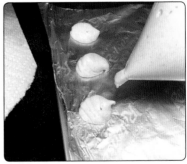

Step 6: Bake

Bake for 10 to 15 minutes or so. Some recipes will end up with the macarons slightly undercooked at the bottom and impossible to remove from the parchment even after cooling. Some recipes tell you to slightly overcook the macarons

so they're dry on the bottom and peel off easily. Then you're supposed to fill your macarons and let them age for a couple of days so the filling can soften the insides of the macarons slightly and bring them to the right texture. Do whatever works best for you. I opted to bake them until I could actually remove them from the pan.

Almond Milk

You can either following the directions for making almond milk here, or you can go to page 2 for a full guide on making almond milk. You can adjust the proportions of almond meal and water, depending on how thick you want your almond milk to be.

go to page 2

INGREDIENTS
- 1 cup water
- 1 cup almond meal

Step 1: Blend and Strain

Add water and almond meal to a food processor or blender. Blend and then strain the milk into a container. Save the pulpy almond for the almond cakes. I had a little less than ¼ cup of almond pulp, which is what I used.

Almond Panna Cotta

Step 1: Prep and Stir

Spray ramekins or teacups (whatever molds you plan on using) lightly with oil. Empty packet of gelatin into a container and stir in the water; let sit 10 minutes until the granules absorb the water.

INGREDIENTS

- 1 packet unflavored gelatin
- 3 Tablespoons water
- 2 cups almond milk
- ¼ cup sugar
- 2–3 drops almond extract, optional

Step 2: Heat and Mix

In a separate dish, heat the almond milk with the sugar in a microwave until the mixture is hot and the sugar is dissolved. Pour the hot liquid onto the gelatin and stir until gelatin is dissolved and thoroughly mixed. Add almond extract, if using.

Step 3: Pour and Chill

Pour the mixture into the individual containers and refrigerate a couple of hours until panna cotta is solidified.

Almond Cakes

INGREDIENTS

- 6 Tablespoons vegan butter
- ¼ cup (or slightly less) pulpy almond left from making almond

- milk
- 1 egg
- ½ cup flour
- ¼ cup sugar
- ¼ teaspoon almond extract

Step 1: Preheat and Prep

Preheat oven to 350 degrees F. Spray a square 8" x 8" or 9" x 9" pan with oil, then line with waxed paper, leaving enough overhang to grab later.

Step 2: Melt and Mix

Melt vegan butter and mix with almond pulp and egg. Stir into flour and sugar, then add almond extract. Spread batter evenly in pan.

Step 3: Bake and Cool

Bake until the middle is just set and the edges are barely starting to turn golden, about 7 to 10 minutes. Let cool, cover pan with another piece of waxed paper, and invert pan to remove the thin cake. Peel off the layer of waxed paper now on top.

Step 4: Divide and Cut Circles

Using a long serrated bread knife, divide the cake into 16 equal squares. Use a round cookie cutter to cut the largest circle possible from each square.

Step 5: Cut More Circles

Use a smaller round cookie cutter to cut a small circle from 8 of the circles, making sure the rings of cake are thick enough that they won't fall apart. Enjoy the scraps, but not all of them right away. Save some for tasting with the chocolate sauce you'll make later!

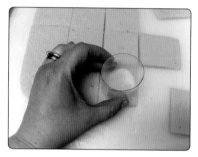 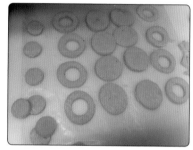

Assemble

Next, we assemble the baked almond cakes, almond cake circles, and apricot preserves. (I prefer the all fruit kind without added sugar so it's not overly sweet.)

Step 1: Warm and Strain

Heat a couple of spoonfuls of apricot preserves in a pan on low until liquefied. Strain into a small container.

Step 2: Paint and Stack

While the apricot preserves are still warm, use a paintbrush to paint a circle border around one of the solid cake circles. Place a cake ring on top. Paint the cake ring with apricot preserves, and top with another cake ring. Repeat with 3 more solid circles and 4 more rings so you have 4 cup-shaped almond cakes with two cake rings stacked on top of a solid bottom.

Step 3: Finish Assembly

Cover each assembled cake with a small piece of waxed paper. Top with the four remaining cake circles, then with one more piece of waxed paper. Using a flat surface like a book, gently press down on the cakes for a minute or two. Watch the cake from the side to make sure you don't crush it.

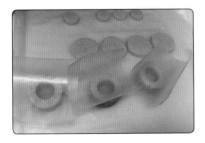

Frozen Cherry Chocolate Foam

Step 1: Melt and Add

Heat the chocolate chips with ½ cup tart cherry juice in a

INGREDIENTS

- ½ cup dark chocolate chips
- 1½ cups tart cherry juice
- ½ teaspoon soy lecithin

container until chocolate is melted. Stir thoroughly. Add remaining cherry juice and soy lecithin.

Step 2: Blend

Using an immersion blender, mix the liquid until a layer of foam forms. Let the container sit for a few minutes so the rest of the dispersed bubbles in the liquid can rise into the foam.

Step 3: Freeze

Spoon the foam into a container and freeze.

Tart Cherry Tapioca Pearls

INGREDIENTS

- ½ cup small tapioca pearls
- 1 cup tart cherry juice
- 1 teaspoon sugar

Step 1: Soak and Add

Soak tapioca pearls in cherry juice and sugar for at least 30 minutes. Pour into a pot and add a couple of cups of water.

Step 2: Cook and Strain

Cook on medium for about 15 minutes, until pearls are no longer hard on the inside. Strain the pearls, rinsing off any excess tapioca goo if necessary.

The Sauces and Fillings

Milk Chocolate Strawberry Sauce

INGREDIENTS

- ¼ cup milk chocolate chips
- 2 medium–large fresh strawberries, chopped
- 2 Tablespoons vegan mascarpone cheese
- 1 pinch soy lecithin

Step 1: Melt and Blend

Melt the chocolate with the strawberries and vegan

mascarpone. Blend thoroughly, add soy lecithin, and blend a bit more, trying to incorporate some bubbles to lighten the sauce a bit.

Macaron Filling

INGREDIENTS

- ¼ cup milk chocolate chips
- 2 Tablespoons milk chocolate strawberry sauce
- 2 Tablespoons vegan butter

Step 1: Melt, Stir, and Spread

Melt the chocolate chips with the sauce and vegan butter. Stir until smooth, cool, and then stir again. Spread the filling between two macaron halves, sandwiching them together. Don't use too much filling or it'll squish out when you bite into the cookie.

Dark Chocolate Cherry Sauce

INGREDIENTS

- ½ cup dark chocolate chips
- ½ cup tart cherry juice
- 2 Tablespoons vegan butter
- pinch soy lecithin

Step 1: Melt, Stir, and Blend

Gently melt the chocolate chips in the cherry juice and vegan butter. Stir well and cool slightly. Add the soy lecithin and blend well, making sure to incorporate tiny little bubbles so the sauce tastes a bit lighter. Pour into a small Ziploc bag. Snip a *very tiny* corner of the bag when ready to pipe the sauce.

Raspberry Mascarpone Filling

INGREDIENTS

- 1 ounce white chocolate
- ¼ cup vegan mascarpone cheese
- ¼ cup fresh raspberries
- 1 teaspoon sugar

Step 1: Grate

Grate 1 ounce white chocolate with a microplane. Add ¼ cup of the grated white chocolate to the vegan mascarpone, raspberries, and sugar in a bowl. Reserve the rest of the white chocolate for garnish.

Step 2: Mash and Stir

Use a fork to mash the raspberries into the other ingredients, and stir well to combine.

Step 3: Fill and Top

Use a spoon to fill the almond cakes with the raspberry mascarpone. Place the tops on the cakes.

Raspberry White Chocolate Sauce

Step 1: Warm and Strain

Heat the remaining raspberry mascarpone filling, then strain it, reserving the liquid and discarding any remaining solids.

How to Plate the Dessert

All the previous steps can be done ahead of time. Plating should be done right before serving.

Step 1: Make a Design

Take your dark chocolate cherry sauce and practice drawing with it, either on a plate or some other surface. (WARNING: Don't turn off safe search if you're doing a Google image search to find inspiration for the chocolate background design, especially if your search includes the word "threesome." Or, if you choose to ignore my advice, don't start drawing on plates after looking at said images!)

Spoon some milk chocolate sauce onto the plate. Pipe dark chocolate sauce on the plate in whatever pattern you like. Abstract or simple patterns are much more likely to please your guests.

Step 2: Decorate the Panna Cotta

Dip the ramekin of panna cotta in some hot water to loosen it, then unmold it onto the plate. Scoop out a little indentation at the top of the panna cotta, and spoon in some tapioca pearls. Top with frozen chocolate foam. You might want to save the frozen foam for the last, possibly even waiting until the plates are on the table, because it melts so quickly. The foam won't lose its shape as it melts, but it won't be frozen any more, and the frozen foam has a really neat texture.

Step 3: Drizzle and Sprinkle

Place the almond cake and the macaron on the plate. Drizzle some warm raspberry white chocolate sauce over the almond cake. Place a fresh strawberry over the pink sauce, then sprinkle on some shaved white chocolate.

Step 4: Final Touch

Shave some milk chocolate over the macaron with a microplane. If desired, slice a strawberry from the tip almost (but not quite) to the stem end. Fan it out and place it on the plate.

Easy Soft-Serve Ice Cream in Less Than 5 Minutes

By maiah03

http://www.instructables.com/id/Easy-Soft-Serve-Ice-Cream-in-Less-than-5-Minutes/

Super easy version of soft-serve ice cream: delicious, fast, *and* healthy!

INGREDIENTS

- 2 frozen bananas
- 1 Tablespoon maple syrup
- 2 teaspoons maca powder
- ½ teaspoon vanilla
- ¼ cup almond milk

Step 1: Food-Process Ingredients

Put all of the ingredients into a food processer and process until fully puréed and blended smooth.

Step 2: Serve Immediately

Divide mixture into 2 bowls and enjoy immediately for the perfect, healthy soft-serve!

 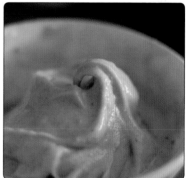

Banana Avocado Pudding

By atepinkrose

http://www.instructables.com/id/Banana-Avocado-Pudding-Vegan-optional/

Ripe bananas . . . sometimes they may not be very appetizing, so we make banana bread—this new, quick, and easy banana avocado smoothie.

INGREDIENTS

- 1 ripe banana
- 1 large avocado or 2 small avocados
- 1 teaspoon of sugar
- 2 cups of almond milk

Step 1: Blend It—Voila!

Blend; if the mixture gets too thick you might have to plunge a wooden spoon at the bottom to get it moving again in the blender.

Step 2: Serve and Enjoy

This will create a thick pudding-like mixture. Note: Use ripe avocados. Ripe avocados are creamy in texture; when squeezed gently, they will feel soft but not mushy and hollow; and they will also have the freshest taste. If still unsure, taste it. It should not be bitter.

Slider Cakes

By nhathy

http://www.instructables.com/id/Slider-Cakes/

Cupcake buns and a brownie patty make up these cute little Slider Cakes! And the best part? They're completely vegan! How ironic! I've seen a lot of cheeseburger cupcake recipes online, but none of them were vegan.

The thought of having someone who was vegan appearing as if they were eating a burger amused me, so I adjusted the recipe.

Surprisingly, there were a few things I've learned about making vegan cupcakes that I thought I'd share. Warning: this takes a lot of time. (For me, because I only have 2 cupcake pans so I had to do a lot of washing in between steps.) It probably took me a total of 2 to 3 hours to make.

Create the Burger Buns

Vegan cupcakes are different from regular cupcakes that use eggs and butter. For one, they don't rise as much as regular cupcakes. Secondly, they don't cut very well. Other cheeseburger cupcake recipes call for you to bake normal cupcakes and then cut through them. This doesn't work with vegan cupcakes. They tend to fall apart and crumble when you try to slice through them. Lastly, they tend to be a little stickier than regular cupcakes. If you don't grease the pan well enough, the cupcakes will burn.**Step 1: Preheat and Prep**

INGREDIENTS

- 1 Tablespoon apple cider vinegar
- 1½ cups almond milk
- 2 cups all-purpose flour
- 1 cup white sugar
- 2 teaspoons baking powder
- ½ teaspoon baking soda
- ½ teaspoon salt
- ½ cup coconut oil, warmed until liquid (or vegetable or olive oil)
- 1¼ teaspoons vanilla extract

Preheat oven to 350°F. Instead of lining your cupcake pans, grease them with a cooking spray.

Step 2: Measure

Measure the apple cider vinegar into a 2-cup measuring cup. Fill with almond milk to make 1½ cups. Let stand until curdled, about 5 minutes.

Step 3: Whisk and Combine

In a large bowl, whisk together the flour, sugar, baking powder, baking soda, and salt. In a separate bowl, whisk together the almond milk mixture, coconut oil, and vanilla. Pour the wet ingredients into the dry ingredients and stir just until blended.

Step 4: Spoon out and Bake

Spoon the batter into the prepared cups, dividing evenly. Make one batch fill up to half the depth of the tray (these are the top buns) and another batch that fills up to a quarter of the tray (these are the bottom buns). Bake until you can poke them with a toothpick and it comes back out clean (about 10 minutes).

Step 5: Cool and Remove

Take them out of the oven and allow them to cool in the pan. Then carefully remove them. I used a fork to scoop them out, but be careful not to scratch the pan! If you try removing the cupcakes before they're cooled enough, they'll break apart.

Create the Burger Patty

Mix the batter for the brownie. You can also just make chocolate cake batter if you don't like brownies. However, I liked the combination of cupcake and brownie.

INGREDIENTS

- 1 cup unbleached all-purpose flour
- 1 cup white sugar
- ⅜ cup unsweetened cocoa powder
- ½ teaspoon baking powder
- ½ teaspoon salt
- ½ cup water
- ½ cup vegetable oil
- ½ teaspoon vanilla extract

Step 1: Preheat and Mix

Make sure your oven is still at 350°F. In a large bowl, stir together the flour, sugar, cocoa powder, baking powder, and salt. Pour in water, vegetable oil, and vanilla; mix until well blended.

Step 2: Spoon Out and Bake

Again, using the cupcake pans, only fill the pans halfway (or less if you want thinner patties). Bake until a toothpick comes clean after poking the center of the brownie (about 15 minutes).

Step 3: Cool and Remove

Allow to cool. Be careful when removing the brownies. They sometimes can break easily.

Make Frosting

Also, if your margarine and/or shortening was refrigerated, I would take it out of the fridge so that it can soften by the time you get to making the frosting.

INGREDIENTS
- ½ cup non-hydrogenated shortening (softened)
- ½ cup non-hydrogenated margarine (softened) (a.k.a. Earth Balance)
- 1½ teaspoons vanilla extract
- ¼ cup plain almond milk
- 3½–5 cups powdered sugar, sifted if clumpy

Step 1: Beat

Beat the shortening and margarine together until well combined and fluffy. This is important. The consistency of your frosting depends on how fluffy you make your shortening and margarine combination.

Step 2: Add and Beat

Add the vanilla and soy milk. Add the sugar and beat until fluffy. Try to make your frosting thicker. To thicken, add more powdered sugar—I'd recommend using around 5 cups total.

Step 3: Prepare Colors

Separate a decent amount of frosting per food coloring that you'd like to make. Mix in enough food coloring until you've reached the desired color. I added in 5 drops at a time. If you don't have frosting bags, you can use Ziploc bags. Cut off the tip of one corner and secure in your frosting tips. Then, scoop in your frosting, making sure not to have the frosting leak through. Next, close the bags, making sure to get rid of as much air as possible.

Step 4: Frost the Bun

Add frosting on the bottom bun. I put the "lettuce" on this layer. I put more of the green frosting on the edges so that it would stick out and can be seen once you put the brownie burger patty on top of it.

Step 5: Add the Patty

Place the brownie burger patty in the center. Add more frosting on top of the burger patty. I put the "cheese" on this layer. I drew a square with the yellow frosting to imitate a slice of cheese.

Step 6: Add the Top Bun

Take the cupcake for the top bun and place it upside-down on top of the brownie burger patty. This keeps the color of the top bun consistent with the bottom bun.

Step 7: Serve and Enjoy!

Optional: Sesame Seeds

You don't really need to do this, but it helps make the slider look more convincing. Some recipes use a lemon or an orange mixture to make the sesame seeds stick. This one uses a simple sugar mixture (1 part water, 2 parts sugar). I like this better because

it doesn't add any additional taste to the cupcake.

Brush some of the mixture on the top of the cupcake and sprinkle some sesame seeds on top.

Ooey-Gooey Chocolate Dessert Crepe

By rvt1985

http://www.instructables.com/id/Ooey-Gooey-Chocolate-y-Dessert-Crepe/

This is my quick and versatile crepe recipe made into a low-calorie, high-protein dessert using chocolate PB2 and a few mini chocolate chips!

INGREDIENTS

CREPE:

- 2 Tablespoons all-purpose flour
- dash of baking powder
- dash of salt
- ½ of one large egg
- 4 Tablespoons of almond milk
- splash of vanilla extract
- ½ Tablespoon of applesauce

FILLING:

- 2 Tablespoons chocolate PB2
- 1 Tablespoon almond milk or water
- a few mini chocolate chips

EQUIPMENT

- lightly greased pan (I used Pam)
- spatula/turner
- fork
- container for leftover egg (unless you're making two crepes)
- small dish for mixing PB2
- medium bowl for mixing crepe

Step 1: Split Your Egg

If you want two crepes, great! If you just want one, I suggest cracking the egg into a small jar and using a fork to whip it into a smooth consistency. Use your thumb to mark half when you're ready to pour the egg into the mixture. Store the other half in the jar for your next crepe.

Step 2: Mix Ingredients

Start with the dry stuff. Mix it around with a fork before you add your half egg, almond milk, splash of vanilla, and applesauce. Mix well to get all the lumps out.

Step 3: Grease and Pour

Lightly grease your pan and put the heat on medium-high for a moment before pouring the batter. Tilt the pan so the batter coats it evenly. You'll know it's time to flip when the edges start to raise up and get a little crispy. This can take between 4 and 6 minutes, but watch closely.

Step 4: Mix the Filling

While you're waiting for the crepe to brown, mix your PB2 according to the package directions, using almond milk instead of water. Add mini chocolate chips as you see fit. Don't have PB2? No problem! The possibilities are

endless. How about real peanut butter, a squirt of Hershey's syrup, or your favorite fruit spread instead?

Step 5: Flip and Fill

Flip your crepe when you see the edges rising up a bit; use your spatula to lift it and make sure it's browning correctly. As soon as you flip it's time to add half of the filling to one quadrant. Fold the crepe in half, then add the second half of your filling over the same spot the first half was added. Fold once more. Press lightly into the pan with your spatula, flip, and repeat.

Step 6: Plate and Serve

Throw that crepe on a plate and garnish with a bit of fresh fruit if you like.

Notes: The same recipe works wonderfully for savory crepes as well, just omit the vanilla and maybe add a grind of fresh cracked pepper instead. I like to make this with a bit of strong cheddar in place of the PB2, served with a side of arugula. It makes a very nice light meal or snack. Make a double recipe for a fat, tasty pancake. It's a little harder to fold but it is fluffy and wonderful. I've also tried this with brie and strawberries for filling, rolled like a burrito . . . it was amazing!

The Healthiest Cupcake in the World

By HeyJBay

http://www.instructables.com/id/The-Healthiest-Cupcake-
in-the-World/

MAKES 8 CUPCAKES

What you are about to learn will change your life forever! No butter, no sucrose, no lactose, and no additional sodium!

Say goodbye to the artery clogging saturated fats, the overused white sugar and salt, the uncomfortable lactose (for those who are lactose intolerant), and say "Hello" to 2½ servings of vegetables and 2½ servings of fruits! That's already a whole day's worth of fruits and vegetables in one batch of the Healthiest Cupcake in the World, while still maintaining that delicious fluffy cupcake sweetness.

INGREDIENTS

- 1 banana*
- 1 kiwi*
- 1 handful blueberries*
- 1 cup baby spinach*
- ¼–½ cup broccoli**
- ¼–½ cup baby carrots**
- 1 cup flour
- 2 eggs
- 1½ teaspoons baking powder
- 1 teaspoon vanilla extract
- 2 Tablespoons sugar-free applesauce
- 1 splash of almond milk

*You can add whatever fruits and vegetables you desire, as long as they make a thick smoothie in the blender.
**Depending on which taste you prefer.

Step 1: Blend

Put all fruits and vegetables in the blender with a splash of almond milk. If you want you can leave out the blueberries for now, and put them in the batter later to have blueberry chunks in the cupcake. Blend the fruits and vegetables. The smoothie should be thick and green, so you may need to add more spinach to get desired "greenness."

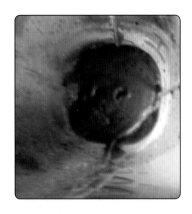

Step 2: Add and Mix

Now add the flour, eggs, powder, vanilla, applesauce, etc. Stir, mix, fold, blend, whatever you desire to make it look like batter.

Step 3: Pour

Pour in some or all of the smoothie (depending on your preferences). Less will make the batter thicker, more will make it thinner.

Step 4: Preheat and Prep

Preheat oven to 350°F. Use Pam for the cupcake pan. Pour batter in to about half to two-thirds full.

Step 5: Bake and Decorate

Cook for 20 minutes. Take out of the oven and enjoy!

I don't really like broccoli too much, and ½ cup was too much for me. Feel free to replace it with whatever you like. Also, the picture shows only

½ cup spinach. I ended up adding an additional ½ cup for additional green color.

I would recommend a butter cream frosting to put on the cakes, but considering I don't have any, I made up a couple of alternatives.

Whipped Cream

Honey Blueberry Glaze

Strawberry Yogurt

Christmas Tree

Homemade Almond Joy Ice Cream

By Henrie Marie

http://www.instructables.com/id/Homemade-Almond-Joy-Ice-Cream-dairy-free-1/

MAKES 2 SERVINGS

Dairy-free, vegan, gluten-free, cholesterol-free, and ice cream maker-free! This recipe came out amazing. The ice cream is creamy and loaded with coconut so it has that dense coconut texture just like the candy bar, and the chocolate hardens once it hits the cold ice cream to form a chocolate shell. Here is what you will need to make this yummy cold treat in your own kitchen, without an ice cream maker.

INGREDIENTS

- 12 Tablespoons cornstarch
- 1¼ cups of almond- and coconut-blended milk
- ¼ cup raw sugar
- ½ can of sweetened cream of coconut (can be found in the cocktail mixer section of your grocery store)
- ½ cup shredded coconut
- slivered or whole plain almonds

CHOCOLATE SAUCE:

- ½ cup dark chocolate chips
- 1 Tablespoon coconut oil

Step 1: Mix

Mix cornstarch with ¼ cup of almond/coconut blend milk. Set aside.

Step 2: Combine and Heat

On medium/high heat, combine one cup of almond/coconut blend milk and sugar. Bring to a boil; this will be ample time for the sugar to melt. Remove from heat and add the cornstarch and almond/coconut milk mixture. Let cool completely.

Step 3: Whip

In a mixing bowl or with a handheld mixer, whip cream of coconut until it is white and forms stiff peaks.

Step 4: Add and Freeze

Add the cooled almond/coconut mixture to the whipped cream of coconut and mix well. Incorporate the shredded coconut flakes into the mixture and transfer to a freezer-safe container. Freeze overnight.

Step 5: Make Sauce

In a double boiler, melt the chocolate chips and coconut oil until silky smooth. Keep at room temperature so it does not harden. It will harden once it comes into contact with cold temperatures.

Step 6: Add Topping

Top the ice cream with almonds and enjoy!

METRIC AND IMPERIAL CONVERSIONS

(These conversions are rounded for convenience)

Ingredient	Cups/Tablespoons/Teaspoons	Ounces	Grams/Milliliters
Butter	1 cup=16 tablespoons= 2 sticks	8 ounces	230 grams
Cream cheese	1 tablespoon	0.5 ounce	14.5 grams
Cheese, shredded	1 cup	4 ounces	110 grams
Cornstarch	1 tablespoon	0.3 ounce	8 grams
Flour, all-purpose	1 cup/1 tablespoon	4.5 ounces/0.3 ounce	125 grams/8 grams
Flour, whole wheat	1 cup	4 ounces	120 grams
Fruit, dried	1 cup	4 ounces	120 grams
Fruits or veggies, chopped	1 cup	5 to 7 ounces	145 to 200 grams
Fruits or veggies, puréed	1 cup	8.5 ounces	245 grams
Honey, maple syrup, or corn syrup	1 tablespoon	.75 ounce	20 grams
Liquids: cream, milk, water, or juice	1 cup	8 fluid ounces	240 milliliters
Oats	1 cup	5.5 ounces	150 grams
Salt	1 teaspoon	0.2 ounces	6 grams
Spices: cinnamon, cloves, ginger, or nutmeg (ground)	1 teaspoon	0.2 ounce	5 milliliters
Sugar, brown, firmly packed	1 cup	7 ounces	200 grams
Sugar, white	1 cup/1 tablespoon	7 ounces/0.5 ounce	200 grams/12.5 grams
Vanilla extract	1 teaspoon	0.2 ounce	4 grams

OVEN TEMPERATURES

Fahrenheit	Celcius	Gas Mark
225°	110°	¼
250°	120°	½
275°	140°	1
300°	150°	2
325°	160°	3
350°	180°	4
375°	190°	5
400°	200°	6
425°	220°	7
450°	230°	8

also available

Awesome Coconut Milk Recipes
Tasty Ways to Bring Coconuts from the Palm Tree to Your Plate

by Instructables.com; Edited and Introduced by Nicole Smith

With Instructables.com's *Awesome Coconut Milk Recipes*, you'll be able to whip up anything from delicious soups to delectable desserts in no time flat! From massaman curry to creepy eyeball panna cotta, these recipes all have one thing in common: the use of coconut milk. This nondairy milk has grown in popularity over the last few years thanks to its rich nutrients and delicious flavor. With this handy guide, the authors of Instructables.com will teach you to make such delightful meals as:

- Green thai chicken curry
- White gazpacho
- Sweet potato ravioli with coconut curry sauce
- (Pi)ña coladas
- Green tea mochi cake
- 100-calorie peanut butter chocolate popsicles
- And many more!

With *Awesome Coconut Milk Recipes*, you could make a three-course meal using coconut milk as a jump-off point. With these recipes, you can get a taste of the tropics in a number of ways, and all of them are delicious!

US $14.95 paperback ISBN: 978-1-62914-755-0

also available

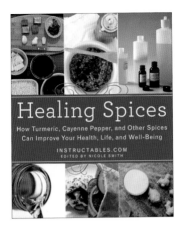

Healing Spices
How Turmeric, Cayenne Pepper, and Other Spices Can Improve Your Health, Life, and Well-Being
by Instructables.com; Edited by Nicole Smith

Spices not only add a flavorful kick to meals; they also have some amazing benefits to improve certain ailments and improve overall health. Rich in antioxidants and polyphenols, spices and herbs like turmeric, cayenne pepper, cinnamon, ginger, garlic, cloves, coriander, and sage can fight inflammation, protect against chronic conditions, and even help with losing weight.

Healing Spices is a great tool for anyone looking to add more flavor to their diet and cut out unhealthy seasonings like salt, sugar, and fatty oils. You'll find great recipes like:

- Chickpea and carrot tagine
- Sweet potato and coconut soup
- Probiotic ginger beer
- Chicken tikka masala with turmeric rice
- Lemon-garlic sorbet
- And many more

There are also remedies for burns, problem skin and hair, losing your voice, and toothaches, as well as a guide detailing the benefits of each spice and herb. *Healing Spices* is the ultimate compendium for anyone wishing to cook with healthier seasonings.

US $14.95 hardcover ISBN: 978-1-62914-815-1

also available

Amazing Cakes
Recipes for the World's Most Unusual, Creative, and Customizable Cakes

by Instructables.com; Edited and introduced by Sarah James

With Instructables.com's *Amazing Cakes*, you'll be able to make cakes shaped like animals, mythical creatures, and vehicles. They may light up, breathe fire, or blow bubbles or smoke. Whether they're cute and cuddly (like a penguin) or sticky and gross (like a human brain!), these cakes have two things in common: they're (mostly) edible and they're amazing!

Instructables.com authors walk you through each step of the process as you cut plywood for cake bases, hardwire figurines for automation, and mix nontoxic chemicals for explosions and eruptions. You'll also learn how to make cakes shaped like:

- Yoda
- Helicopters
- 3-D dinosaurs
- Moving tanks
- Pi signs
- Bass fish
- Zombie heads
- Swimming pools
- Ladybugs
- Evil clowns
- And more!

US $12.95 paperback ISBN: 978-1-62087-690-9

also available

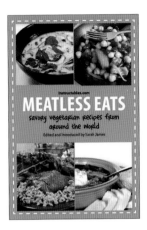

Meatless Eats
Savory Vegetarian Recipes from Around the World
by Instructables.com; Edited by Sarah James

Originating from Instructables, a popular project-based community made up of all sorts of characters with wacky hobbies and a desire to pass on their wisdom to others, *Meatless Eats* gives full step-by-step instructions for creating delicious vegetarian dishes that even die-hard carnivores will crave. Written by cooks who can't get enough of veggies, each recipe contains pictures for an easy follow-along guide, even for those who spend little to no time in the kitchen. Discover your inner vegetarian with these mouthwatering recipes:

- Eggplant Parmesan
- Veggie mexican lasagna
- Portobello mushrooms with grilled feta burger
- Scrumptious caponata
- Tomato frittata
- Fiery pumpkin samosas
- Vegetarian mushroom gravy
- And many more!

The Instructables community offers a great mixture of tastes and cuisines. Italian, Mexican, American, and more will appease any picky eater as well as provide for those who are willing to try just about anything.

US $12.95 paperback ISBN: 978-1-62087-697-8